Grammar and Punctuation

Grammar 6 Teacher's Guide

Carol Matchett

Schofield & Sims

Free downloads available from the Schofield & Sims website

A selection of free downloads is available from the Schofield & Sims website (www.schofieldandsims.co.uk/free-downloads). These may be used to further enhance the effectiveness of the programme. The downloads add to the range of print materials supplied in the teacher's guides. They include the following items:

- a **Curriculum coverage chart**
- an enlarged **Focus text** for each lesson
- a **Dictation assessment sheet**
- a **Pupil target reminder**
- a **Learning pathways class chart** for each year group
- a **Final test analysis class chart** for each year group.

Published by **Schofield & Sims Ltd**, 7 Mariner Court, Wakefield, West Yorkshire WF4 3FL, UK
Telephone 01484 607080
www.schofieldandsims.co.uk

This edition copyright © Schofield & Sims Ltd, 2017
First published in 2017
Second impression 2018

Author: **Carol Matchett**
Carol Matchett has asserted her moral rights under the Copyright, Designs and Patents Act, 1988, to be identified as the author of this work.

British Library Cataloguing in Publication Data
A catalogue record for this book is available from the British Library.

Design by **Oxford Designers & Illustrators Ltd**

Printed in the UK by **Page Bros (Norwich) Ltd**

ISBN 978 07217 1401 1

Contents

Introduction

Schofield & Sims Grammar and Punctuation is a structured whole-school scheme for teaching grammar and punctuation while also building on vocabulary, reading and writing skills. It can be used alongside the **Schofield & Sims Spelling** series for complete Spelling, Punctuation and Grammar [SPaG] coverage.

Grammar and Punctuation is designed to progressively develop knowledge and understanding of grammatical concepts through six teacher's guides and six pupil books containing a carefully structured sequence of lessons. The teacher's guides provide you, the teacher or adult helper, with notes and activities to support the teaching of these lessons, annotated answers to the pupil book questions, and a variety of assessment resources for tracking progress.

Supporting a mastery approach, the focus of this programme is on rich practice, deep and secure understanding and fluency in application. Pupils not only learn the terminology and correct usage of grammar and punctuation, but they also build up the skills, knowledge and confidence to apply them in their own independent writing. All pupils are encouraged to move at the same pace through the lessons and are given the same opportunity to fully understand the concept being taught. A wealth of practice questions, writing tasks, activity ideas and resources are provided to support the wider application of the grammar and punctuation that has been learnt in each lesson and to help pupils to truly master the art of writing.

The programme is designed primarily for pupils in Years 1 to 6, and the concepts and terminology that are introduced are in line with the National Curriculum for English. However, understanding of grammar and punctuation is cumulative, so grammatical terms and concepts introduced in one book are revisited and developed further in subsequent books to reinforce the pupils' understanding. In particular, concepts and areas of learning introduced towards the end of one book are revisited and embedded in the next book to further ensure consolidation and continuity.

There are 30 corresponding lessons in **Grammar 6** and its related **Teacher's Guide**, ten for each term. These lessons follow the statutory requirements for Year 6 'Vocabulary, grammar and punctuation' in the National Curriculum for English including Appendix 2, while also promoting and supporting other aspects of the English curriculum. A curriculum coverage chart is available to download from the Schofield & Sims website. An extended glossary can also be found at the back of this teacher's guide [pages 91–96], with a full list of all the terminology relevant to the Year 6 curriculum, along with clear explanations, examples and lesson references.

IMPLEMENTING THE TEACHING MODEL

The **Grammar 6 Teacher's Guide** supports explicit teaching of grammar and punctuation within the wider teaching of reading, writing and speaking. It is based around focused teaching sessions, using the following pedagogical model:

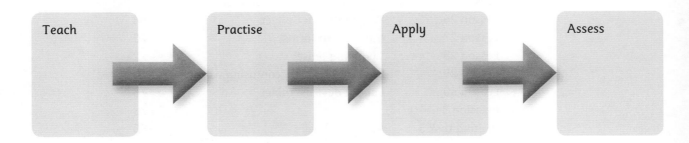

Teach → Practise → Apply → Assess

USING THE TEACHING NOTES

This teacher's guide supports an approach to teaching grammar and punctuation that is systematic, thorough and direct. The teacher's guide provides you with detailed **Teaching notes** for each lesson. A sample page is included below to show the structure of a typical lesson.

Teaching notes

Schofield & Sims **Grammar and Punctuation** | Grammar 6 Teacher's Guide

Lesson 1 **Subordinate clauses**

Focus using a range of subordinate clauses to clarify, elaborate and link ideas effectively

Key terms main clause, subordinate clause, adverbial, relative clause, conjunction, relative pronoun

Focus text Slowly, the door slid open. Peering through the visor of my helmet, I stepped out into a new, unexplored world. My space boots sank into the soft grey powder that covered the surface of the planet. Even though I was excited, I was trembling inside my space suit.

TEACH

Show the focus text. Read it aloud and discuss the clues about the setting, character and events in the story. Discuss how this detail is given through the use of noun phrases, adverbials and subordinate clauses.

Remind the pupils that subordinate clauses help to expand and link ideas in our writing by adding more information to a main clause. Ask the pupils to identify the subordinate clauses used in the focus text and discuss how they expand on the main clause.

Recap the different types of subordinate clause. For example, a subordinate clause functioning as an adverbial [e.g. Even though I was excited, I was trembling ...] begins with a subordinating conjunction and can be added before or after the main clause. A relative clause begins with a relative pronoun and gives more information about a noun [e.g. powder that covered the surface ...].

Ask the pupils to find the sentence beginning with a verb [Peering through the visor ...]. Underline it and explain that this is another type of subordinate clause, which is useful for providing variety in writing. An –ing clause is always separated from the main clause by a comma. [Note: Traditionally, a clause was required to include a finite verb, e.g. 'I was peering', but now non-finite clauses are also recognised. The pupils do not need to know this terminology.]

Remind the pupils that single-clause sentences are also useful in writing. Ask them to identify the one in the focus text [Slowly, the door slid open.]. Discuss why it was used [e.g. for effect; it creates suspense].

EXTEND Discuss other clauses starting with verbs [e.g. To reach the base, ...; Excited at the thought, ...]. Point out that these clauses are also separated from the main clause by a comma.

PRACTISE

Pupil book page 4

APPLY

- The pupils write a short paragraph or opening for a story using a range of subordinate clauses.
- When reading together, collect sentences with subordinate clauses to use as models for writing.
- In narrative writing, the pupils use subordinate clauses to show links, relationships and contrasts.
- Remind the pupils to edit their writing, checking that sentences link together correctly.

ASSESS

Dictation: Leo sat at his desk. He had not written a word. It was history but he was not interested today.
Say: Rewrite each sentence, adding a subordinate clause.
Answer: e.g. Leo sat at his desk as he gazed into the distance. Although it was nearly the end of the lesson, he had not written a word. It was history, which was his favourite subject, but he was not interested today.
Check: The sentence punctuation is correct throughout, including commas.

10

The learning objective of the lesson.

Terminology that the pupils will encounter in the lesson.

A short focus text for use at the start of the lesson.

Detailed lesson notes offering guidance on how to teach a specific grammatical feature or concept.

Extension of the lesson focus for pupils who want to explore further.

Reference to the relevant pupil book page, which contains practice activities to develop understanding.

A dictation activity to assess learning.

Ideas and activities for applying the concept in speech and independent writing.

TEACH

Each lesson begins with an introductory panel featuring the following information:

- **Focus** – The focus of the lesson is clearly stated.
- **Key terms** – The key terminology to be used in the teaching session is listed. Any new terminology that the pupils will come across for the first time in that lesson is highlighted in bold.
- **Focus text** – A short focus text is provided that has been designed for use at the start of the lesson. It is intended that the focus text is written or projected on to a whiteboard to be shared with the pupils. The focus texts cover a range of genres of writing and help to provide a context for the learning that allows the pupils to appreciate the purpose or effect of the target grammar or punctuation feature. All the focus texts are available to download from the Schofield & Sims website.

Clear guidance is given on how to use the **Focus text** at the start of the lesson to 'focus in' on the particular grammar or punctuation feature that you are teaching. The **Teaching notes** suggest possible ways that you can explain, demonstrate and discuss the feature to develop understanding. Sessions often involve some oral composition or shared writing, with the pupils involved in suggesting ideas and correcting mistakes.

The main teaching session covers the objectives that are required for the pupils to work at the expected standard, but there is also a suggestion for how you can **Extend** the focus for pupils who have grasped the main concept and are ready to delve deeper. These suggestions often provide a bridge to later lessons in the programme.

PRACTISE

Following the teaching session, the pupils are ready to practise the grammar or punctuation feature that has been introduced and clear page references are provided for the corresponding lesson in the pupil book. This provides the pupils with rich practice activities to consolidate their learning. The pupils can work individually or in pairs. In paired work, discussion between partners can help to develop understanding, encourage thoughtful answers and promote oral rehearsal.

At the top of each pupil book page a **Remember** panel provides a child-friendly summary of a key learning point from the lesson with examples that refer back to the **Focus text**. This acts as a reminder for the pupil and is also a useful reference for parents if sections of the pupil book are set as homework.

In **Grammar 6**, there are three pupil book activities for each lesson. The first **Try it** activity is designed to check that the pupils understand the key learning point; the second is designed to develop and use this understanding within sentences. You could do some of the activities orally, with the class or in groups, before the pupils write their answers. Each lesson then ends with a **Sentence practice** activity where the pupils compose their own sentence or sentences using the concept that has been taught in the lesson. If a pupil requires additional challenge, the **Sentence practice** could be extended by increasing the number of sentences required. A sample page from the pupil book is provided on page 7. It shows the structure of a typical page and some of the main features.

As the pupil book is completed, it will form an ongoing record of the pupil's progress. It will also be a useful reminder for the pupil when writing independently.

Answers to all the pupil book activities are provided in the teacher's guide. Alongside the answers you will also find detailed annotations offering guidance on what to look out for and how to tackle potential problems, as well as suggestions for discussing or comparing the pupils' answers.

There are **Revision** pages at the end of each section of the pupil book. In **Grammar 6**, these pages revise concepts introduced in earlier books as well as material from earlier sections of the current book, making sure that learning is not forgotten. The focus of each revision activity is given on the **Answers** pages in the teacher's guide to help you identify areas where the pupils might need further revision.

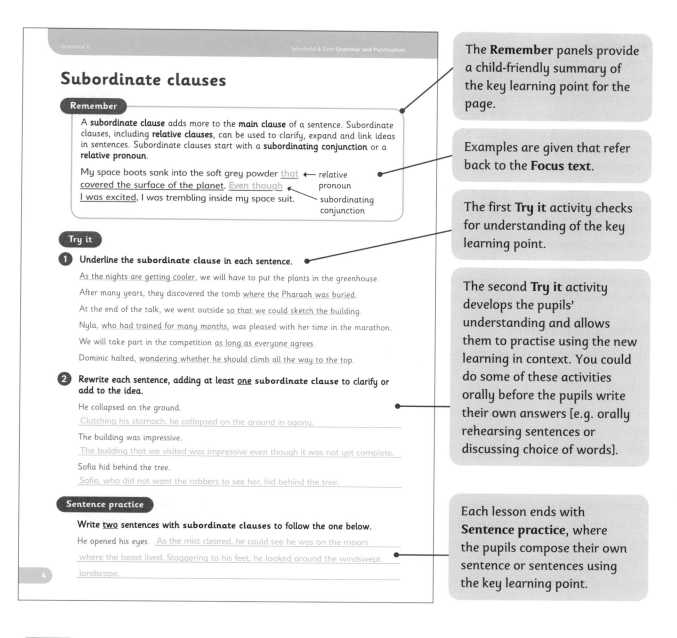

The **Remember** panels provide a child-friendly summary of the key learning point for the page.

Examples are given that refer back to the **Focus text**.

The first **Try it** activity checks for understanding of the key learning point.

The second **Try it** activity develops the pupils' understanding and allows them to practise using the new learning in context. You could do some of these activities orally before the pupils write their own answers [e.g. orally rehearsing sentences or discussing choice of words].

Each lesson ends with **Sentence practice**, where the pupils compose their own sentence or sentences using the key learning point.

APPLY

A challenge when teaching grammar and punctuation is ensuring that pupils transfer learning from grammar lessons into their own writing. This is why the **Teaching notes** always provide a list of suggestions for activities where the pupils might apply their new learning in written, or sometimes oral, composition. These opportunities may be in English lessons or across the curriculum. You can use these suggestions as and when appropriate and you should also look for opportunities to embed learning in the writing activities you already have planned.

It is important to establish the expectation that what has been taught and practised in a grammar and punctuation lesson is applied when writing. This can be helped by setting targets for writing that relate to a specific grammar and punctuation concept that has been taught, and referring to these before, during and after writing, especially in marking and feedback. You will find further support for target-setting on page 9.

At the end of each section of the pupil book there is a short **Writing task**. This again helps to make explicit the link between the grammar and punctuation lessons and the pupils' own writing. The **Writing task** provides an opportunity for the pupils to apply, or 'show off', what they have learnt about grammar and punctuation by using it in written composition. It can be used as a starting point for further creative writing or topic-based activities. There is more information about how to use and assess the **Writing task** on page 8.

ASSESS

Regular assessment is crucial to check understanding, reflect on learning and monitor progress. It is important that teachers know what the pupils have learnt, what they are finding difficult and what they need to know next. This helps inform teaching, planning and target-setting. **Grammar 6** and its related **Teacher's Guide** offer frequent opportunities and a range of resources for in-school assessment, which can be used flexibly in line with your own school's assessment policy.

Ongoing assessment

At the end of each page of the **Teaching notes** you will find a short assessment task based around a dictation exercise. This is designed to be used once the pupils have completed the relevant lesson in the pupil book and begun to apply the new learning in their writing. The pupils are required to write and punctuate dictated sentences. They are often then asked to change or annotate the sentences in some way, following verbal prompts. This dictation task is designed to show whether the pupils have understood the terminology and the key learning objective of the lesson. Sometimes previous learning is also checked. A **Dictation assessment sheet** is available to download from the Schofield & Sims website.

Periodic assessment

The **Writing task** at the end of each section in the pupil book allows for a more formal assessment of how the pupils are applying their cumulative knowledge of sentence structure, grammar and punctuation in their own writing.

At Key Stage 2, the writing tasks require pupils to write for different purposes and in different forms. You can remind the pupils that you will be looking at their choices of vocabulary, grammar and punctuation but do not give any further help or examples of sentences, words or phrases that might affect the assessment. Allow the pupils a few minutes' planning time to note down their ideas before they begin writing.

Included in the teacher's guide is an **Analysis sheet** for each **Writing task** [pages 32, 56 and 80]. This lists relevant criteria relating to punctuation, and to grammar and sentence structure, based on what has been taught to date. Look for each criterion in the pupil's completed **Writing task** and record whether there is no evidence, some evidence or clear evidence of the use of that feature in the piece of writing. Photocopies of these sheets can also be used to analyse other samples of writing to give a better picture of a pupil's abilities.

Also included is a **Pupil checklist** for each **Writing task** [pages 33, 57 and 81]. This is designed to encourage the pupils' self-assessment and also allows you to give targeted feedback. As the pupils complete the checklist you could ask them to annotate their writing to show where they have successfully used a particular grammar or punctuation feature [e.g. circling the conjunctions they have used].

Whether you choose to use the **Analysis sheet** or the **Pupil checklist**, both sheets include a space for you to record a future target for the pupil. This is an important part of the writing assessments: identifying strengths and weaknesses and informing future teaching. Any problems or misunderstandings that are noted should be addressed and targets updated based on the evidence.

Summative assessment

There is a **Final test** provided as a photocopiable resource on pages 82–85 of this teacher's guide. This is designed to be used as an end-of-year assessment when all or most of the sections of the pupil book are complete. It is similar in style to the short answer test in the end of Key Stage 2 National Tests and it covers all the content introduced in the programme. You can use it to help check the pupils' learning and whether their progress is in line with expectations.

A **Mark scheme** for the **Final test** is provided on pages 86–87 and gives the answers and assessment focus of each question. The **Analysis sheet** for the **Final test** allows you to record the pupils' marks and will be helpful in identifying individual or class strengths and areas that might need to be revisited. This can be found on page 88 and a whole-class version is available to download from the Schofield & Sims website.

Tracking progress

A number of resources are provided at the back of the teacher's guide and as downloadable resources to further support assessment of learning, tracking progress and record-keeping.

Following a **Writing task**, if a group of pupils require further focused support on a particular writing target, the **Target tracking sheet** on page 89 can be used to note evidence of progress towards that target. You should look for evidence of progress in independent writing in English and in other subjects. Judgements should not be made solely on one piece of writing.

Pupil name	Evidence from independent writing	Progress in independent writing		
Sarah Jacobs	Paragraph on 'My family'. Book review of 'The Nightingale'. Science report on 'Habitats'.	①	②	③

The target should be reviewed after a set period of time to see if it has been achieved. A new target might then be set, or further teaching and reinforcement opportunities planned as necessary. A **Pupil target reminder** is available to download from the Schofield & Sims website. This can be placed on a pupil's desk as a prompt to remind them of their current writing target.

The **Learning pathways sheet** on page 90 acts as an at-a-glance overview of where a pupil is in their learning. If completed at regular intervals [e.g. at the end of every term] it allows you to track the progress that has been made and to identify areas where further support might be needed. Alternatively, it can be completed just once at the end of the year to act as a useful summative record for the pupil's subsequent teacher. The chart shows criteria in line with the expected standards for Year 6. Circles are ticked to show the depth of a pupil's understanding. These judgements should be made using a variety of evidence, including a number of examples of independent writing. Learning is only definitely embedded when the concept is always or nearly always present, based on evidence from a range of writing tasks. A **Learning pathways class chart**, available to download from the Schofield & Sims website, allows you to keep a record of progress for the whole class in one spreadsheet.

The pupils should also be encouraged to reflect on their own learning at regular intervals, saying what they have learnt and how they have used it in their writing. There is a **Progress chart** at the back of the pupil book where the pupils can record their progress through the programme by ticking the circle when they feel they have achieved the content of the statement.

Lesson 1 Subordinate clauses

Focus using a range of subordinate clauses to clarify, elaborate and link ideas effectively

Key terms main clause, subordinate clause, adverbial, relative clause, conjunction, relative pronoun

Focus text Slowly, the door slid open. Peering through the visor of my helmet, I stepped out into a new, unexplored world. My space boots sank into the soft grey powder that covered the surface of the planet. Even though I was excited, I was trembling inside my space suit.

TEACH

Show the focus text. Read it aloud and discuss the clues about the setting, character and events in the story. Discuss how this detail is given through the use of noun phrases, adverbials and subordinate clauses.

Remind the pupils that subordinate clauses help to expand and link ideas in our writing by adding more information to a main clause. Ask the pupils to identify the subordinate clauses used in the focus text and discuss how they expand on the main clause.

Recap the different types of subordinate clause. For example, a subordinate clause functioning as an adverbial [e.g. Even though I was excited, I was trembling ...] begins with a subordinating conjunction and can be added before or after the main clause. A relative clause begins with a relative pronoun and gives more information about a noun [e.g. powder that covered the surface ...].

Ask the pupils to find the sentence beginning with a verb [Peering through the visor ...]. Underline it and explain that this is another type of subordinate clause, which is useful for providing variety in writing. An –ing clause is always separated from the main clause by a comma. [Note: Traditionally, a clause was required to include a finite verb, e.g. 'I was peering', but now non-finite clauses are also recognised. The pupils do not need to know this terminology.]

Remind the pupils that single-clause sentences are also useful in writing. Ask them to identify the one in the focus text [Slowly, the door slid open.]. Discuss why it was used [e.g. for effect; it creates suspense].

EXTEND Discuss other clauses starting with verbs [e.g. To reach the base, ...; Excited at the thought, ...]. Point out that these clauses are also separated from the main clause by a comma.

PRACTISE

Pupil book page 4

APPLY

- The pupils write a short paragraph or opening for a story using a range of subordinate clauses.
- When reading together, collect sentences with subordinate clauses to use as models for writing.
- In narrative writing, the pupils use subordinate clauses to show links, relationships and contrasts.
- Remind the pupils to edit their writing, checking that sentences link together correctly.

ASSESS

Dictation: Leo sat at his desk. He had not written a word. It was history but he was not interested today.
Say: Rewrite each sentence, adding a subordinate clause.
Answer: e.g. Leo sat at his desk as he gazed into the distance. Although it was nearly the end of the lesson, he had not written a word. It was history, which was his favourite subject, but he was not interested today.
Check: The sentence punctuation is correct throughout, including commas.

Pupil book answers

Subordinate clauses

Remember

A **subordinate clause** adds more to the **main clause** of a sentence. Subordinate clauses, including **relative clauses**, can be used to clarify, expand and link ideas in sentences. Subordinate clauses start with a **subordinating conjunction** or a **relative pronoun**.

My space boots sank into the soft grey powder <u>that</u> ← relative <u>covered the surface of the planet</u>. <u>Even though</u> ← pronoun <u>I was excited</u>, I was trembling inside my space suit. ← subordinating conjunction

Try it

1 Underline the **subordinate clause** in each sentence.

<u>As the nights are getting cooler</u>, we will have to put the plants in the greenhouse.

After many years, they discovered the tomb <u>where the Pharaoh was buried</u>.

At the end of the talk, we went outside <u>so that we could sketch the building</u>.

Nyla, <u>who had trained for many months</u>, was pleased with her time in the marathon.

We will take part in the competition <u>as long as everyone agrees</u>.

Dominic halted, <u>wondering whether he should climb all the way to the top</u>.

2 Rewrite each sentence, adding at least <u>one</u> **subordinate clause** to clarify or add to the idea.

He collapsed on the ground.

Clutching his stomach, he collapsed on the ground in agony.

The building was impressive.

The building that we visited was impressive even though it was not yet complete.

Sofia hid behind the tree.

Sofia, who did not want the robbers to see her, hid behind the tree.

Sentence practice

Write <u>two</u> sentences with **subordinate clauses** to follow the one below.

He opened his eyes. As the mist cleared, he could see he was on the moors where the beast lived. Staggering to his feet, he looked around the windswept landscape.

4

This example shows how the pupils might use subordinate clauses to give detail or link ideas. Look for varied structures and the use of relative clauses and/or –ing clauses as well as those starting with subordinating conjunctions. Check that commas have been used after fronted subordinate clauses.

The questions include different types of subordinate clause, which you could discuss with the pupils [e.g. clauses starting with subordinating conjunctions, relative pronouns, non-finite verbs].

They also show subordinate clauses in different positions. The pupils could use them as models.

Check that the pupils do not mistake main clauses, or phrases acting as adverbials [e.g. After many years; At the end of the talk], for subordinate clauses.

These are just examples. They show different types of subordinate clause used in different positions. Compare the pupils' answers to see which ones develop the original sentence most effectively.

These examples show the minimum required. Sentences could be developed further by adding adverbials or another clause.

Check the use of commas after fronted subordinate clauses, and any parenthesis.

Lesson 2 Relative clauses

Focus using relative clauses to clarify, define and add detail

Key terms relative clause, relative pronoun, noun, main clause, comma, parenthesis

Focus text The gods <u>who lived on Mount Olympus</u> ruled the world.
Apollo, <u>who was the son of Zeus</u>, was responsible for the sun's movement across the sky.
Poseidon, <u>the brother of Zeus</u>, was god of the sea.
Hera was the goddess <u>who married Zeus and became queen</u>.
The hydra was a monster <u>that had many heads</u>.
The hydra was a many-headed monster, <u>which was killed by Hercules</u>.

TEACH

Show the focus text. Read and discuss the information given about Greek gods.

Discuss what type of subordinate clause is used in these sentences [relative clause – beginning with the relative pronouns 'who', 'which', 'that', and giving more information about a noun]. Point out that in the sentence about Poseidon, the relative pronoun 'who' has been omitted.

Explain that some relative clauses give information about a noun that is not essential. For example, the relative clauses about Apollo and Poseidon add an extra detail as a parenthesis. Without it, the rest of the sentence still makes sense and tells us who they were. In this situation, commas are used to show the parentheses and separate the relative clause from the main clause.

Compare this to the sentence about Hera. Explain that here the relative clause is essential to the sentence because it specifies *which* goddess Hera was [the goddess who married Zeus]. Explain that no commas are used if a relative clause tells us something essential about the noun.

Discuss the two sentences about the hydra. In the first sentence, the relative clause gives essential information that clarifies 'a monster', so there is no comma. In the second sentence, the relative clause adds an extra piece of information, so a comma is needed to separate it from the main clause.

EXTEND Use the sentence about Mount Olympus to discuss how commas can change the meaning of sentences like this. Add commas before and after the relative clause and discuss the effect on meaning. [Note: This topic is covered in more detail in Lesson 25.]

PRACTISE

Pupil book page 5

APPLY

- Discuss the use of embedded relative clauses in newspaper reports to give extra information about people and events. The pupils use the same technique when writing their own newspaper reports.
- The pupils use relative clauses in stories to clarify and give extra information about characters and settings [e.g. Joe was a tall boy, who ...; He took them to the place where ...].

ASSESS

Dictation: Marston Woods was a place <u>where few people ever went</u>. The path <u>that led through the woods</u> was overgrown. Local villagers, <u>who were timid folk</u>, preferred to take the long way round.
Say: Underline the relative clauses.
Check: The sentence punctuation is correct, including the parenthesis.

Pupil book answers

Relative clauses

Remember

A **relative clause** gives more information about a **noun**. When the information is essential to your meaning because it helps to clarify <u>which</u> noun, no comma is used to separate it from the main clause.

The hydra was a monster <u>that had many heads</u>.

When the information just gives an extra detail, one or two commas are used to separate it from the main clause.

Apollo, <u>who was the son of Zeus</u>, was responsible for the sun.
The hydra was a many-headed monster, <u>which was killed by Hercules</u>.

Try it

1 Complete each sentence by adding a **relative clause** that helps to clarify the **noun** with essential information.

It was the village chief <u>who</u> <u>had three daughters.</u>

The stomach is the place <u>where</u> <u>food is digested.</u>

Kavita was a beautiful princess <u>who</u> <u>lived in India hundreds of years ago.</u>

He had these enormous eyes <u>that</u> <u>stared back at you.</u>

Harvest is the time <u>when</u> <u>farmers gather in their crops.</u>

2 Complete each sentence by adding a **relative clause** with extra information that is not essential.

I could see the serpent's head_____, which was sticking up out of the trees.

The caretaker_____, who will retire this year,_____ has worked here for thirty years.

Kieran Cooper revisited his old school_, which brought back lots of happy memories.

The artefacts_____, which were very interesting,_____ came from the museum.

Mrs Khan_____, whose daughter is in my class,_____ gave a cookery demonstration.

Sentence practice

Write <u>two</u> sentences about an escaped tiger. Use both types of **relative clause** in your sentences.

The tiger that escaped from the zoo has been seen in the park. The tiger, which could be dangerous, was seen close to the children's play area.

5

These are just examples of relative clauses that could be used to clarify the noun. Compare the pupils' answers, discussing how they specify the person, thing, place or time. Answers for factual sentences are likely to be similar to those shown, although there could be variation [e.g. Harvest is the time when people celebrate gathering in their crops.].

These are just examples of extra information that could be added to the main clause. Compare the pupils' answers to see what extra information has been added.

Where the relative clause is added as a parenthesis, check that another comma has been added after it.

These are just examples. The relative clauses could be used to give detail about places or people rather than the tiger [e.g. A zoo keeper who has been specially trained ...].

Check that commas [or brackets or dashes] have been used to indicate a parenthesis or non-essential clause added at the end of a sentence.

Lesson 3 Active voice

Focus using the terms 'active voice', 'subject' and 'object' in relation to sentences

Key terms **active voice**, **subject**, **object**, verb, noun, noun phrase, pronoun

Focus text Dad filled the bucket. He climbed the ladder. As he reached the top, he dropped the bucket of water. The bucket hit the floor. The water drenched poor Isla. Mum heard her scream. She opened the back door. The door nudged the ladder.

TEACH

Show the focus text and read it aloud. Discuss the sequence of events and the likely consequences.

Explain that these sentences are written in the active voice. This means that the *subject* of the sentence [who or what the sentence is about] performs the action expressed by the verb. Ask the pupils to identify the subject and verb in each sentence. Circle the subject and underline the verb. In each sentence, the subject comes before the verb. Point out that the subject of the sentence can be a noun [e.g. Dad; Mum], a noun phrase [e.g. The bucket; The water] or a pronoun [e.g. He; She].

Explain that in these sentences there is also someone or something that 'receives' the action, or has the action done to it. This is called the *object* of the sentence. Ask the pupils to identify the object in each sentence [e.g. the bucket; the ladder]. Again, it can be a noun, a noun phrase or a pronoun. Make sure the pupils understand that, in the technical or grammatical sense, the object of a sentence can be a person as well as a thing [e.g. 'The water drenched poor Isla.' – Isla receives the drenching from the water].

Explain that sentences normally follow this pattern of subject–verb–object. Invite the pupils to orally compose another sequence of sentences following this pattern – for example, based on the focus text but changing the subject, verb and/or object [e.g. A monkey climbed a tree. He ate a ripe banana. He dropped the banana skin.].

EXTEND Choose a passage from a book and identify sentences written in the active voice.

PRACTISE

Pupil book page 6

APPLY

- The pupils write their own humorous sequence of events for a story. They use the active voice to describe actions [e.g. The mouse taunted the cat but then the cat chased the mouse.].
- The pupils write an adventure story with an exciting, high-action sequence of events. They use the active voice to highlight actions [e.g. Something hit Max. He grabbed a large stick.].
- The pupils write headlines using the active voice [e.g. Man sees UFO.].
- Discuss the use of the active voice in descriptive writing [e.g. to describe the actions of a storm or the sea – 'The waves tossed the boats …'].
- The pupils write 'subject–verb–object' sentences linked to other school subjects [e.g. The Vikings invaded Britain.].

ASSESS

Dictation: The thieves grabbed the money. The woman behind the counter pressed the alarm. A passer-by chased the thieves down the road.

Say: Underline the subject of each sentence. Then circle or highlight the object of each sentence.

Pupil book answers

Active voice

Remember

The **subject** of a sentence is who or what the sentence is about. In the **active voice**, the subject <u>performs</u> the action stated in the **verb**. The person or thing that <u>receives</u> the action is called the **object**.

<u>Dad</u> dropped <u>the bucket of water</u>. <u>The water</u> drenched <u>Isla</u>.
  ↑   ↑   ↑   ↑   ↑   ↑
subject verb   object   subject verb object

Try it

1 Read each sentence. Write whether the **subject** or **object** is underlined.

<u>The woodcutter's mighty axe</u> struck the tree.	subject
The police stopped <u>the red car</u> at the traffic lights.	object
The hurricane destroyed <u>the beachside resort</u>.	object
<u>He</u> raised the glass to his lips.	subject
The woman on the motorcycle delivered <u>the pizzas</u>.	object
<u>The river</u> flooded the surrounding fields.	subject

2 Rewrite each sentence with a different **subject** and **object** but the same **verb**.

The waiter poured the coffee.	Mum poured the milk.
The traffic blocked the road.	An elephant blocked the motorway.
He destroyed the sandcastle.	The angry girl destroyed the letters.
Lightning struck the tall tree.	The batsman struck the cricket ball.
The dog licked my cheek.	The little girl licked her ice lolly.
Vegetables provide vitamins.	Houses provide shelter.

These are just examples of sentences using the same verb but changing the subject [or 'do-er'] of the action and the object [or receiver] of the action. The pupils could use nouns, noun phrases or pronouns in their sentences. Compare the pupils' answers.

Sentence practice

Write <u>two</u> sentences in the **active voice**. Use the word 'cushion' as the **subject** in the first sentence and the **object** in the second sentence.

subject   A cushion hit Jamie's head.

object   Lauren threw the cushion.

6

These are just examples of sentences using the word 'cushion' as the subject and as the object.

Lesson 4 Passive voice

Focus introducing and using the passive voice to change the focus of a sentence

Key terms active voice, **passive voice**, subject, object, verb

Focus text **Flames lit up the night sky. Without thinking, Eric grabbed the fire extinguisher. He flung open the door. Immediately, Eric was choked by thick smoke. He was forced back by the flames.**

TEACH

Read the focus text. Discuss the events [e.g. What is Eric trying to do? Will he succeed?]. Look at the first three sentences again. Recap that these are written in the active voice – the subject of the sentence is the person or thing doing the action [Flames, Eric, He]. The sentences also have an object, or 'receiver' of the action. Underline the object in each sentence [the night sky, the fire extinguisher, the door]. Show that it comes *after* the verb, and that the sentences follow the pattern subject–verb–object.

Read the last two sentences. Discuss who/what *performs* the actions in these sentences [the smoke, the flames] and who/what *receives* the action [Eric]. Underline the receiver [Eric, He], to show that the receiver of the action is at the start of the sentence, *before* the verb – it is now the subject of the sentence.

Explain that this type of construction is called the passive voice – the subject of the sentence is the 'passive' person or thing that receives the action. The 'do-er' is then called the agent and is tagged on to the end of the sentence, using the word 'by' [by <u>thick smoke</u>, by <u>the flames</u>]. [Note: The pupils do not need to know the term 'agent', but you may find it useful to introduce it.]

Discuss the effect of using the passive voice [e.g. it keeps the focus on Eric; it emphasises the effect of the actions on him rather than focusing on the thing doing the action]. Work with the pupils to rewrite one of the active sentences as a passive sentence [e.g. The night sky was lit up by flames.]. Discuss the changes needed [e.g. moving the object to the start of the sentence; adding the auxiliary verb 'was' before the verb; using 'by' to add the do-er or agent after the verb].

Explain that sometimes the do-er or agent is not included if it is unknown, or if the sentence would be more effective without it. Together, orally compose some examples and the questions they lead to [e.g. 'The building was set on fire.' – Who was responsible?; 'Eric was struck on the head.' – By what?].

EXTEND Discuss past participle forms used in passives [e.g. The windows were <u>broken</u> by the fire.].

PRACTISE

Pupil book page 7

APPLY

- When the pupils are writing stories, encourage them to occasionally use the passive voice to keep the focus on a character [e.g. to show how events affect them; to suggest helplessness].
- In narratives, encourage the pupils to write passive sentences sometimes without the agent, to hide who is responsible and to create mystery or suspense [e.g. The light was switched on.].
- The pupils write newspaper reports using passives where the do-er is not known or not important [e.g. The door was forced open. The wolf was killed.].
- The pupils use passives to write about investigations in science [e.g. The mirror was placed …].

ASSESS

Dictation: I saw the accident on my way home. A car hit a lamppost. <u>The police were called.</u> A lady helped the driver out of the car. <u>The accident was probably caused by an icy road.</u>

Say: Underline the sentences written in the passive voice.

Pupil book answers

Passive voice

Remember

To write a sentence in the **passive voice**, you turn the active sentence around so that the **object** (the person or thing that <u>receives</u> the action) becomes the **subject**. An **auxiliary verb**, such as '**was**', should be added before the main verb.

Active voice

<u>Thick smoke</u> choked <u>Eric</u>.
   ↑   ↑
 subject   object

Passive voice

<u>Eric</u> was choked by <u>thick smoke</u>.
 ↑   ↑
subject   object

Try it

1   Read each sentence and write whether it is in the **active** or **passive voice**.

The documents were examined by an expert.   *passive*

This magnificent cake was made by Elena's mother.   *passive*

The mayor opened the new shopping centre.   *active*

The prime minister signed the agreement yesterday.   *active*

The rocket was propelled into the air.   *passive*

The invaders attacked the castle walls.   *active*

2   Rewrite each sentence so that it is written in the **passive voice**.

The referee postponed the game.   <u>The game was postponed (by the referee).</u>

A tap on the window surprised them.   <u>They were surprised by a tap on the window.</u>

Photographers surrounded the film star.   <u>The film star was surrounded by photographers.</u>

Bad weather delayed our flight to Spain.   <u>Our flight to Spain was delayed (by bad weather).</u>

Qualified instructors teach the children.   <u>The children are taught by qualified instructors.</u>

Sentence practice

Write <u>two</u> sentences in the **passive voice** to describe the effects of a storm.

<u>Trees were blown over by the gales. Roofs were damaged by the strong winds.</u>

Remind the pupils to look for clues in the construction of the sentence [e.g. the use of 'was'/'were' before the verb].

In the fifth sentence, the agent [or 'do-er'] of the action is not included. If necessary, discuss this with the pupils – something must have 'propelled' the rocket but it is not included because the focus is on the rocket.

The pupils may omit the agent [by ...] from the sentence and in some cases this may be the better option. You could discuss the effect of omitting the do-er of the action with the pupils.

Also discuss how changing the sentences from active to passive affects the focus of the sentence [e.g. by putting the focus on the film star rather than the photographers].

These are just examples of possible sentences using the passive voice. The pupils may choose to omit the added 'by ...' phrase. Compare sentences and discuss how using the passive voice puts the focus on the results of the storm.

Lesson 5 Colons and semicolons in lists

Focus using a colon to introduce a list and semicolons within a list

Key terms comma, **colon**, **semicolon**, punctuation

Focus text **This pizza has all my favourite toppings: spicy pepperoni, red onions, red peppers, sliced tomatoes and extra mozzarella cheese. There was a choice of four puddings: apple pie, which was my choice; a chocolate dessert with a gooey centre; strawberry cheesecake; and ice cream in a choice of flavours.**

TEACH

Show the first sentence of the focus text. Ask the pupils to read it and count the toppings on the pizza. Discuss the use of commas to clearly separate the items in a list. Ask the pupils to think about how this list sentence is different from list sentences they have seen or written before.

Explain that this sentence uses a punctuation mark called a colon to introduce the list. When we use a colon to introduce a list, the part of the sentence before the colon must make sense by itself – it is a main clause. Orally compose another sentence using a colon to introduce a list [e.g. The cereal bars come in several delicious flavours: ...].

Show the second sentence and read it aloud. Discuss the choice of puddings. Ask the pupils what is different about this list sentence. Explain that this sentence uses punctuation marks called semicolons rather than commas to separate the items in the list.

Explain that we use semicolons rather than commas when a list is made up of longer phrases, particularly if any of those phrases contain other punctuation marks such as commas, as this helps to avoid confusion. Point out that in the focus text a semicolon has also been used before the word 'and' for clarity – it is not 'strawberry cheesecake <u>and</u> ice cream in a choice of flavours', as these are two separate options. However, usually no semicolon is needed before 'and'.

Ask the pupils to compose their own list of puddings or other items, punctuated with semicolons.

EXTEND Explain that commas, too, can be used before the word 'and' if it helps to avoid ambiguity [e.g. ..., apple pie and custard, and ice cream].

PRACTISE

Pupil book page 8

APPLY

- When writing information texts, the pupils use a colon to introduce a list of examples [e.g. Many animals could soon be extinct: tigers, pandas ...].
- In other subjects, the pupils use sentences with lists to give a number of pieces of information succinctly [e.g. component parts; features of locations – 'The area has many natural resources: ...'].
- The pupils write descriptive sentences made up of expanded noun phrases and punctuated with colons and semicolons [e.g. Inside, there was the Captain's hidden treasure: doubloons of gold; ...].
- When writing stories, the pupils set the scene by using a sentence with a list of verb phrases [e.g. In the castle courtyard everyone was busy: servants rushing here and there; ...].

ASSESS

Dictation: Please bring the following items for the party: a selection of sandwiches on white and brown bread; small cakes, which should not contain nuts; fresh fruit salad; and orange or apple juice.
Check: All punctuation is correct, including the semicolon before the final 'and' to avoid ambiguity.

Pupil book answers

Colons and semicolons in lists

Remember

A **colon** is used at the end of a clause that introduces a list. If the list includes longer **phrases**, **semicolons** rather than **commas** should be used to separate them – particularly if the phrases already contain other punctuation marks. You should only use a semicolon before 'and' if it is needed to clarify the meaning.

There was a choice of four puddings: apple pie, which was my choice; a chocolate dessert with a gooey centre; strawberry cheesecake; and ice cream in a choice of flavours.

Try it

1 Insert a **colon** and **semicolons** in the correct places in each sentence.

Wood is used to make many items: the furniture in our houses; flooring; sports equipment, such as hockey sticks and cricket bats; musical instruments and even children's toys.

There are five oceans: the Pacific Ocean, the largest and deepest; the Atlantic Ocean, which separates America and Europe; the Indian Ocean; the Arctic Ocean and the Southern Ocean.

We bundled the shopping into the car: bags stuffed with groceries; a huge box of washing powder, which we almost left behind; cartons of milk and juice; and a toy donkey.

2 Complete each sentence, using **semicolons** in your list.

I have packed everything in my rucksack: a waterproof coat, which is essential; my camera and spare film; a pair of socks (just in case); a bottle of water and my packed lunch.

David has travelled to many countries: Kenya, which he has visited many times; Japan, where he worked for a while; Australia, to visit his brother; and, most recently, China.

Sentence practice

Write a sentence that includes a list of friends and a detail about each one. Use <u>one</u> **colon** and at least <u>one</u> **semicolon**.

I have three best friends: Guy, who I sit next to in class; Finn, who I walk to school with; and Freya, who lives next door.

8

Although a semicolon is not strictly necessary when 'and' is used to add the last item, a semicolon is sometimes helpful in complicated lists to avoid ambiguity [e.g. when the item preceding it contains the word 'and' or when 'and' could join it to the preceding phrase].

These are just examples of how the pupils might continue the sentences. Check that there is no capital letter after the colon or semicolon unless for a proper noun.

Encourage the pupils to use at least some longer phrases in their list. Remind them that this is the reason for using semicolons rather than commas.

This is just an example of a possible sentence. Check that there is an independent introductory clause before the colon. Remind the pupils to add some detail about the friends to form longer phrases, rather than just giving a list of names. Point out that a simple list of names could be separated with commas.

Lesson 6 **Bullet points**

Focus using and punctuating bullet points to list information

Key terms **bullet points**, punctuation, colon, comma, semicolon, full stop, capital letter

Focus text Bullet points can be useful in the following texts:
- a leaflet
- a set of instructions
- an on-screen presentation

TEACH

Show the focus text. Ask the pupils to describe how it is presented [e.g. as bullet points; each item is on a separate line, preceded by a 'bullet point']. Discuss why we sometimes present information as bullet points rather than in a sentence [e.g. it makes the items in a list very clear so it is easier for the reader to follow].

Ask the pupils to suggest some other texts where bullet points could be used. Add these suggestions to the focus text as additional bullet points. You could also discuss where it is not appropriate to use bullet points [e.g. in a story].

Explain that there is no one correct way of punctuating a list of bullet points, but that the important thing is that the punctuation is consistent. Before the list begins, there is an introductory clause, which ends with a colon – as with a list sentence.

Point out that in the focus text, the items in the list are phrases, not full sentences, so no punctuation has been used at the start or end of each bullet point. As the list starts like this, it must be maintained throughout. Sometimes commas or semicolons are used at the end of each bullet point. If we start the list using commas or semicolons, it is important to continue using them until we add the last item. The last item should then end with a full stop.

Point out that sometimes bullet points are complete sentences. In this case, we usually start each item with a capital letter and end it with a full stop. Semicolons are also sometimes used rather than full stops, but then a full stop is used after the last item. Again, consistency is the key thing to remember.

EXTEND Discuss other ways of presenting information [e.g. tables; columns], and when these might be used.

PRACTISE

Pupil book page 9

APPLY

- The pupils use consistently punctuated bullet points when writing instructions [e.g. a list of items needed – phrases; a list of steps to complete – full sentences].
- Encourage the pupils to look for opportunities to include bullet points within a range of information texts [e.g. leaflets; booklets; posters].
- Ask the pupils to use bullet points to report back on items raised in group discussions [e.g. on screen or on a flipchart].

ASSESS

Dictation: You might see a number of birds of prey, such as buzzards, kestrels, eagles or red kites.
Say: Present this information as a list with bullet points.
Answer: 'You might see a number of birds of prey:' with four bullet points and no 'or'.
Check: The bullet-point punctuation is consistent.

Pupil book answers

Bullet points

Remember

Bullet points can be used to present a list of information. The introductory clause usually ends with a **colon**. There is no single correct way of punctuating a list of bullet points, but the important thing is that the punctuation is <u>consistent</u> throughout.

Try it

1 Add more information to each list. Punctuate your **bullet points** consistently.

For a healthy diet, include foods from each of these food groups:

- carbohydrates, such as bread and cereals;
- proteins, such as meat and fish;
- fruit and vegetables, which have lots of vitamins;
- milk and dairy;
- some fats.

At Green Acres Adventure Centre you can try many exciting activities:

- orienteering
- rock climbing
- zip wire
- kayaking
- archery

2 Write a **bullet point** list that shows the information from the sentence below.

To make a Caribbean fruit salad, the recipe says you need a ripe mango, a papaya, two satsumas and a tablespoon of brown sugar.

To make a Caribbean fruit salad, you will need:

- a ripe mango
- a papaya
- two satsumas
- a tablespoon of brown sugar

Sentence practice

Write a **bullet point** list giving ideas on how to save water. Punctuate it consistently. Write your list on a separate piece of paper.

These are just examples of information that might be added.

The first item is shown with no capital letter at the start but a semicolon at the end, so the other items should have the same punctuation, apart from the last item, which should end with a full stop.

These are just examples of activities that might be added.

This time the first item is shown with no capital letter and no end punctuation, so the other items should follow the same pattern.

Check that there is an independent introductory clause ending with a colon.

The punctuation used for the bullet points must be consistent.

The list of bullet points should begin with an independent introductory clause ending with a colon. The pupils may have chosen to punctuate their bullet points in different ways, but the punctuation used must be consistent throughout.

9

Lesson 7 Synonyms

Focus understanding how words are related by meaning as synonyms

Key terms **synonym**, adjective, verb, noun

Focus text To help you stay healthy, we serve healthy meals made with healthy ingredients.

We were happy to be home.
The team's supporters were happy after the victory.

The brave knight walked towards his trusty horse ready to ride bravely into battle.

TEACH

If possible, provide the pupils with a thesaurus to use during the lesson. Remind them that a thesaurus gives lists of synonyms. Synonyms are words that have the same or similar meanings. Some words have lots of synonyms but not all have exactly the same meaning. Show this by reading one or two entries from the thesaurus. Explain that when we choose synonyms, we must think about how we want to use them.

Show and read the first sentence of the focus text. Discuss why we might want to use synonyms here [to avoid repeating the word 'healthy']. Explain that the word 'healthy' is used to describe both a person and foods. Ask the pupils to find or suggest synonyms to describe healthy foods or ingredients [e.g. wholesome; nourishing; nutritious]. Use these to improve the sentence.

Show the two sentences containing the word 'happy'. Discuss why synonyms would improve these sentences [e.g. to clarify *how* happy they are]. Ask the pupils to suggest a synonym for 'happy' to fit each sentence, showing different levels of happiness [e.g. glad to be home; ecstatic after the victory].

Show the final sentence. Discuss why we might want to use synonyms in this sentence [e.g. to avoid repetition but also to use more interesting or literary vocabulary]. Point out that verbs and nouns, as well as adjectives, often have synonyms. Invite the pupils to suggest synonyms for different words in the sentence, explaining how these would enhance it [e.g. The gallant/valiant knight marched/strode towards his trusty steed ready to gallop fearlessly into battle.].

EXTEND Explore which kind of words have the most synonyms [e.g. adjectives with shades of meaning].

PRACTISE

Pupil book page 10

APPLY

- The pupils plan a piece of writing on a given subject or theme. As part of the planning, they use a thesaurus to find and note useful synonyms for words related to the theme.
- When they are writing, encourage the pupils to orally compose sentences, trying out synonyms before they write. Remind them to think about how their choices change and enhance meaning.
- Ask the pupil to improve a completed piece of writing by replacing words with synonyms.
- 'Ban' obvious words [e.g. good], so that the pupils have to find more precise synonyms to use in different contexts and types of writing.

ASSESS

Dictation: On Sunday, Ben was <u>very</u> late going to bed so he was <u>extremely</u> tired the next morning. His mum called him <u>several</u> times but Ben had <u>many</u> reasons for staying in bed that day.
Say: Underline the two words in each sentence that are synonyms of each other.

Pupil book answers

Synonyms

Remember

Synonyms are words that have the same or very similar meanings.

We serve healthy meals made with nutritious ingredients.

A thesaurus gives lists of synonyms for words – for example, you will find lots of synonyms for the word 'happy'. However, not all synonyms of a word have exactly the same meaning.

We were glad to be home.　　The team's supporters were ecstatic.

Try it

1 Draw a line to match words that are **synonyms** of each other.

immediate — instant
childish — immature
important — significant
enough — sufficient
havoc — chaos
persuade — convince

The pupils could use a thesaurus or a dictionary to help them with this activity if necessary.

2 Write a **synonym** of the underlined word that could be used in the sentence.

It tasted really <u>horrible</u>.　　repulsive

In the rush to the exit, I was <u>pushed</u> out of the way.　　jostled

The path to the summit was <u>dangerous</u>.　　treacherous

Her jokes and stories began to <u>annoy</u> me.　　irritate

The robot's head <u>turned</u> round.　　swivelled

There is a <u>roomy</u> kitchen at the back of the house.　　spacious

The pupils may have made different choices. Compare their answers, discussing why each word was chosen [e.g. Does it make the meaning clearer? Is it more precise? Does it enhance the effect – perhaps sounding more horrible/more dangerous?].

Encourage the pupils to refer to a thesaurus when selecting synonyms.

Sentence practice

Write <u>two</u> sentences about a grandmother, using **synonyms** of the words 'funny', 'jolly' and 'friendly'.

Our grandmother is very amiable. She is a jovial character who tells the most hilarious stories.

10

These are just examples of sentences using some synonyms of the given words. The pupils may have chosen different synonyms or used them in different ways.

Lesson 8 Antonyms

Focus understanding how words are related by meaning as antonyms

Key terms synonym, **antonym**, prefix

Focus text Grogan Greyheart was a mean, cantankerous, sneaky wizard, who was hostile to everyone he met.
Wenlock Whitebeam was a generous, good-natured, honest wizard, who was friendly to everyone he met.

TEACH

Show the first sentence of the focus text. Read it aloud and discuss the character of Grogan. Identify the words that describe his character, underlining the adjectives [mean, cantankerous, sneaky, hostile]. Discuss possible synonyms for these words [e.g. miserly; bad-tempered; sly; unfriendly].

Show the second sentence and read it aloud. Discuss the very different character of Wenlock and underline the adjectives used to describe him. Compare the underlined words in the two sentences. Ask the pupils what they notice [they are opposites] and highlight each pair of adjectives.

Explain that words that have opposite meanings are called antonyms, the opposite of synonyms. Point out that some words have more than one possible antonym [e.g. another antonym for 'friendly' is 'unfriendly']. Remind the pupils that prefixes such as un–, dis–, and in– can be added to words to create new words with opposite meanings.

Point out that a thesaurus often includes antonyms as well as synonyms. They are usually given after the list of synonyms. Invite the pupils to suggest some more pairs of antonyms that could be used in sentences to describe Grogan and Wenlock, using a thesaurus if required [e.g. gloomy/merry; unfeeling/considerate].

Discuss antonyms of verbs and nouns to use in the descriptions as well as adjectives [e.g. snubbed/welcomed; frown[ed]/smile[d]; enemies/friends].

EXTEND Investigate which kinds of words have more antonyms [e.g. adjectives] and which have none [e.g. some nouns].

PRACTISE

Pupil book page 11

APPLY

- The pupils create two contrasting characters, using antonyms to describe them [e.g. reliable/untrustworthy].
- The pupils write stories with contrasting settings or moods. They use antonyms to make these contrasts clear [e.g. After the noisy kitchen, the peaceful garden was a relief.].
- Encourage the pupils to identify antonyms in other subject areas [e.g. inhale/exhale; transparent/opaque; soluble/insoluble; urban/rural; developed/undeveloped; war/peace].
- The pupils write poems using antonyms for effect [e.g. by writing verses contrasting war and peace; day and night].

ASSESS

Dictation: Diwali is a celebration of <u>good</u> defeating <u>evil</u> and <u>light</u> triumphing over <u>darkness</u>. It recalls the time when Rama and Sita <u>returned</u> home to their kingdom, many years after they <u>left</u>.
Say: Underline the words in each sentence that are antonyms of each other.

Pupil book answers

Antonyms

Remember

Antonyms are words that have opposite meanings.

Grogan Greyheart was a <u>mean</u>, <u>cantankerous</u>, <u>sneaky</u> wizard.
Wenlock Whitebeam was a <u>generous</u>, <u>good-natured</u>, <u>honest</u> wizard.

Try it

1 Underline the **antonym** of each word in **bold**.

transparent	solid	<u>opaque</u>	flexible	frozen
predictable	superior	hospitable	preferable	<u>unexpected</u>
assist	<u>hinder</u>	interfere	evade	direct
important	discreet	fortunate	<u>insignificant</u>	empty
encourage	discover	<u>dissuade</u>	succeed	permit
permanent	particular	frivolous	original	<u>temporary</u>

The pupils could use a dictionary or thesaurus to help them with this activity, if required.

2 Complete each sentence using <u>two</u> words that are **antonyms** of each other.

This ___famous___ piece of music was written by a composer who was ___unknown___ .

If I ___send___ you this parcel in the post, will you be there to ___receive___ it?

Cotton is a ___natural___ material but nylon is a ___synthetic___ fabric.

The first attempt was a ___success___ but the second attempt was a ___failure___ .

The doctors hope that his condition will ___improve___ and not ___worsen___ .

The accused said that he was ___innocent___ but the judge decided he was ___guilty___ .

The pupils may have completed the sentences with other pairs of antonyms. These are acceptable as long as they make sense in the context.

Sentence practice

Write a sentence using the word 'attach' and its **antonym**.

Detach the entry form at the bottom of the page and attach it to your painting.

11

This is just an example of a sentence using the two words 'attach' and 'detach'. Although 'detach' is the more obvious synonym of 'attach', you could accept similar words given in a thesaurus [e.g. unfasten].

Lesson 9 Standard English

Focus recognising non-Standard words and expressions used in spoken language

Key terms Standard English, non-Standard English, verb form, pronoun, apostrophe

Focus text "There be something fishy goin' on next door," said Mrs Twig, from behind the twitching curtains of Number 6, Chestnut Avenue. "Them kids is up to no good."
"They ain't pinching me spuds again, is they?" said Mr Twig, leaving the comfort of his armchair. "I know it were them what done it. I'll nip out an' nab 'em."

TEACH

Show the focus text and read it aloud using appropriate expression for the two characters.

Remind the pupils that when we write we usually use Standard English. Discuss why the writer has chosen to use words and expressions that are non-Standard English in this extract [e.g. to create two interesting characters; to make the direct speech sound natural or local].

Ask the pupils to identify examples of non-Standard English phrases used by the characters. Discuss the use of non-Standard verb forms [There be, kids is, ain't, is they, it were, done it] and pronouns in place of determiners [e.g. them kids; me spuds]. Identify examples of slang or colloquial words and phrases [e.g. fishy; pinching; spuds; nip; nab]. Remind the pupils that these would not normally be used in writing.

Discuss the use of apostrophes to show the omission of letters, when replicating how words are shortened in normal speech. Explain that some of these, although informal, are acceptable Standard English [e.g. I'll], while others are non-Standard English [e.g. goin'; 'em].

Together, rewrite Mr and Mrs Twig's conversation using only Standard English forms [e.g. "There seems to be something rather strange going on next door," ...]. Once complete, read the two versions and compare the effect [e.g. the new version sounds more formal].

EXTEND Write a similar conversation, replicating local spoken forms and using colloquial expressions.

PRACTISE

Pupil book page 12

APPLY

- The pupils write a story, deliberately using non-Standard English in direct speech to show character [e.g. two young children speaking together; a family gathering].
- In pairs, the pupils act out or orally compose a dialogue between a character using non-Standard English and an authority figure using Standard English [e.g. pupil and head teacher]. They then write the scene as a script, replicating the non-Standard forms.
- Invite the pupils to listen to recordings of people using informal speech. They then try to replicate what was said in writing.

ASSESS

Dictation: The police nicked them robbers what pinched the gold bars. They'd hid the gold but was trying to ditch the bags. The gold must be stashed somewhere near 'ere.
Say: Underline the non-Standard English words. Then rewrite the passage using Standard English.
Answer: The police caught those robbers who stole the gold bars. They had hidden the gold but were trying to get rid of the bags. The gold must be hidden somewhere near here.

Pupil book answers

Standard English

Remember

Standard English is nearly always used in writing. However, in **informal** speech, people sometimes use non-Standard English words and expressions.

"They're not stealing my potatoes, are they?" said Mr Twig.   (Standard English)
"They ain't pinching me spuds, is they?" said Mr Twig.   (non-Standard English)

Try it

1 Underline the words that are non-**Standard English**.

"I <u>ain't</u> <u>gonna</u> tell you again," said Granddad. "Take <u>them</u> noisy games and <u>buzz off</u>. I'm <u>havin'</u> a <u>kip</u>."

"I've got this <u>dead</u> good idea for the show," said Mia. "It's <u>gonna</u> be <u>well</u> <u>cool</u>."

I read about a <u>bloke</u> in the paper <u>what</u> won a million <u>quid</u> and then <u>blew</u> it in a year.

"I <u>done</u> it!" shouted Ruby, proudly waving her swimming certificate. "It <u>were</u> a <u>doddle</u>. Is <u>yous</u> proud of me?"

I've <u>gotta</u> go now <u>'cos</u> <u>me</u> mum's calling me. It <u>were</u> good talking to <u>yer</u>.

"<u>Them</u> swings <u>is</u> <u>real</u> dangerous," said Ian. "Ali <u>busted</u> his arm but it could <u>of</u> <u>bin</u> worse."

2 Rewrite the sentence so that it uses only words that are **Standard English**.

It's right nippy in 'ere, innit? <u>It's really cold in here, isn't it?</u>

All me mates was there 'cept Dan. <u>All my friends were there except Dan.</u>

There ain't nowt to see 'ere. <u>There is nothing to see here.</u>

What are yous on about? <u>What are you talking about?</u>

Them kids ain't done owt. <u>Those children haven't done anything.</u>

I'm shattered so let's just chill out. <u>I'm exhausted so let's just relax.</u>

Sentence practice

Write at least <u>two</u> sentences of **direct speech** between two characters using non-**Standard English**.

<u>"I ain't half 'ungry," said Lisa. "Shall we get some grub?"</u>

<u>"I fancy some of them sandwiches. They was wicked," said Luke.</u>

Discuss why the words are not Standard English and what the Standard English version of the sentence would be.

The sentences should be correctly punctuated, including apostrophes, commas and question marks.

Correctly spelt and punctuated contractions of verbs are acceptable as Standard English, although they are informal [e.g. It's]. [Note: The pupils will learn more about formal and informal language in the next lesson, Lesson 10, and in Lessons 11 and 12.]

This is just an example of some direct speech using non-Standard English. The direct speech should be punctuated correctly with inverted commas and other punctuation.

Lesson 10 Formal and informal vocabulary

Focus comparing the vocabularies of informal speech/writing and formal speech/writing

Key terms **formal**, **informal**, Standard English

Focus text I am writing to complain about the pencil case I bought recently. I only got/purchased it on Saturday and the zip has already broken. This is not good enough/unacceptable. I hope you will be able to fix/rectify the problem. You could/It may be possible to replace the zip. Otherwise, I think you should replace/I hope you will consider replacing the pencil case.

TEACH

Show the focus text. Read the first sentence and discuss the purpose and audience for the letter [e.g. a letter of complaint to the manufacturer of the pencil case, or the shop where it was bought].

Remind the pupils that it is important to use the right language for the specific audience or situation. Formal language is needed when speaking or writing to someone official whom we do not know, as in the focus text. Formal language shows that we think the situation is important, and in some situations using formal language is more likely to gain respect and cooperation.

Read the rest of the letter, inviting the pupils to select the formal word or phrase from those highlighted. Underline these choices. Once complete, read aloud the formal version of the letter.

Then read the letter with the alternative choices. Explain that these words are still Standard English words and phrases but they are informal or less formal than the words we use in formal writing. Discuss how the informal choices tend to be shorter words [e.g. got; fix] and ones that we use in everyday speech [e.g. not good enough]. Formal choices tend to be longer, more complex words and phrases that we do not use in normal speech [e.g. purchased; unacceptable; rectify].

Explain that formal speech and writing also require polite language that we might not use informally [e.g. 'I hope you will consider' rather than 'I think you should']. Invite the pupils to orally compose more sentences for the letter, continuing to use formal language.

EXTEND Discuss linking adverbials used in more formal texts [e.g. nonetheless; henceforth].

PRACTISE

Pupil book page 13

APPLY

- The pupils write letters of complaint, for real or imaginary situations, using formal language to gain the respect and cooperation of the reader. They use a thesaurus to help them make suitable word choices.
- The pupils role-play situations requiring formal language in speech.
- Together, read examples of formal writing [e.g. letters; notices; information leaflets]. Make lists of formal words and their informal equivalents for the pupils to refer to when planning writing.
- Make use of any opportunities for the pupils to write for a real official or unknown audience.
- When editing, encourage the pupils to change words to maintain a formal style.

ASSESS

Dictation: I thought the quality of the food was unacceptable. The portion size was OK but the presentation was extremely unappealing. Furthermore, the meal was cold on arrival.
Say: Underline the informal word and suggest a more formal alternative.
Answer: e.g. reasonable

Pupil book answers

Formal and informal vocabulary

Remember

Different words and phrases are used in **formal** and **informal** situations. Formal language is needed when speaking or writing to someone official or to someone you do not know.

Informal

I only got it on Saturday.
This is not good enough.

Formal

I only purchased it on Saturday.
This is unacceptable.

Try it

1 Complete the tables with words that could be used in a **formal** situation.

Informal	Formal
find out	discover
get	obtain
need	require
ask for	request
show	demonstrate

Informal	Formal
live at	reside
help	assist
go ahead	proceed
a hold-up	a delay
enough	sufficient

There are other words that could be used as formal choices.

The pupils could use a thesaurus to help them with this activity.

2 Rewrite each sentence using words that are more suitable for **formal** writing.

It would be great if you could come to our do and we hope you'll think about it.

It would be an honour if you could attend our celebration and we hope you will consider it.

I reckon we can stop people spoiling the park and make it a better place.

I believe that we can prevent people from ruining the park and improve the outdoor space.

Please be sure that all your things have the right labels on them.

Please ensure that all personal possessions are correctly labelled.

These are examples of sentences using more formal vocabulary. The pupils might find it useful to think about examples of formal writing they have read, or to imagine themselves in a formal role [e.g. head teacher].

Compare the pupils' answers and discuss which sound most formal.

Sentence practice

Write two or three sentences about returning an item to a shop, using **formal** words and phrases.

I hope you will consider my request to exchange this item. I did obtain a receipt when I purchased the item. Unfortunately, I seem to have misplaced it.

13

This is just an example showing how the pupils might demonstrate the use of formal language choices.

Revision 1 answers

This page revises punctuation from **Grammar 4** and **5**. The pupils should now be using these punctuation marks independently in their writing as well as proofreading their work to check that they are used correctly.

The focus of each activity is given to help identify areas that may need reinforcement.

Focus: punctuating direct speech

Mrs Marshall's spoken words should be punctuated as one sentence, while Becky's words should be punctuated as two.

Revision 1

1 Rewrite these sentences, punctuating them as **direct speech**.

Let's make a start said Mrs Marshall and Becky can join in when she's ready.

I'm ready now said Becky, dragging up a chair. I've finished tidying up.

"Let's make a start," said Mrs Marshall, "and Becky can join in when she's ready."

"I'm ready now," said Becky, dragging up a chair. "I've finished tidying up."

Focus: apostrophes for possession; plural –s and possessive –'s

The use of apostrophes with plural –s is a common problem. Check for this when the pupils are writing independently.

2 Each sentence has at least <u>one</u> incorrect use of an **apostrophe**. Write the sentences correctly.

The teams' are ready for Saturday's final.   The teams are ready for Saturday's final.

Who's going to Megans' party?   Who's going to Megan's party?

Peoples' homes were flooded.   People's homes were flooded.

Both castle's tower's are 400 years old.   Both castles' towers are 400 years old.

Focus: punctuation to indicate parenthesis

If necessary, remind the pupils that the brackets go around the extra information in the sentence. The words outside the brackets should still make a complete sentence.

When rewriting, the pupils may use either dashes or commas in the first sentence, but dashes are a better choice in the second, as the parenthesis already contains a comma.

3 Insert a pair of **brackets** in the correct place in each sentence.

Matthew (who had been ice-skating before) made it look easy.

I made a poster (quite a good one, in fact) to advertise our campaign.

Rewrite the sentences above using a different punctuation mark instead of brackets.

Matthew, who had been ice-skating before, made it look easy.

I made a poster – quite a good one, in fact – to advertise our campaign.

4 Circle the incorrect use of a **comma** in the passage below.

For a long while, he continued to climb the rocky path. It couldn't be much further now, could it? Suddenly, he heard a noise, he whipped round. Staring out from a hole in the mountainside, he saw two jet black eyes.

Explain why it is incorrect.

'He heard a noise' and 'he whipped round' are both main clauses, so the comma should be a full stop.

14

Focus: using full stops [not commas] to demarcate sentence boundaries

Remind the pupils that a comma cannot be used to separate two independent main clauses. Commas can only separate main clauses and subordinate clauses. [Note: The use of the semicolon to separate main clauses is covered in Lesson 17.]

Schofield & Sims **Grammar and Punctuation**

Grammar 6

5 Underline the **main clause** in this sentence.

One day after tea, when everyone was watching television, <u>he slipped out of the back door</u>.

Rewrite the sentence above using a different **subordinate clause**.

One day after tea, while his father was washing the dishes, he slipped out of the back door.

6 Add another **main clause** to each sentence. Use a different **co-ordinating conjunction** each time.

Ben was a sheepdog but he didn't like sheep.

The train arrived and people climbed aboard.

Millie knew she must stop crying or the other girls would laugh at her.

7 Add words before and after each noun to make an **expanded noun phrase**.

a flat   a basement flat in a big old house

a cellar   a musty cellar with giant cobwebs

the pool   the filthy pool of polluted water

8 Rewrite this sentence, adding an **adverbial** that is a **phrase** to the start of it. Punctuate the sentence correctly.

He was feeling better.   Within a few days, he was feeling better.

9 Change the wording of this statement to make it into a **question** and then an **exclamation**.

It was a terrible mistake.

question   Was it a terrible mistake?

exclamation   What a terrible mistake!

10 Rewrite this sentence, adding a **subordinate clause** that gives a condition.

We will have some free time on Friday.

If you behave well this week, we will have some free time on Friday.

15

This page focuses on the formation of sentences by combining words, phrases and clauses. It revises sentence terminology introduced in earlier books, which will be useful in Section 2 when the pupils learn more about punctuation between clauses.

Focus: main and subordinate clauses

If necessary, remind the pupils that the main clause makes sense independently. The rewritten sentence shown is just an example. Any correctly punctuated sentence with a different subordinate clause is acceptable. Check that the subordinate clause is changed and not the fronted adverbial [a phrase].

Focus: co-ordinating conjunctions and main clauses

Any correctly punctuated sentence using 'or', 'and' or 'but' to add another main clause is acceptable.

Focus: expanded noun phrases

These are just examples. Discuss the pupils' answers.

Focus: fronted adverbials

This is just an example. Check that the fronted adverbial is followed by a comma.

Focus: conditional sentences

This is just an example. If the subordinate clause begins the sentence, a comma should be added.

Focus: sentence types

The pupils can use question words, question tags or reverse the word order to form the question. It must end with a question mark. The pupils may just add an exclamation mark to make an exclamatory statement. However, the question asks them to change the *wording*. This means that the answer needs an exclamation that starts with 'What' or 'How'.

Writing task 1: Analysis sheet

Pupil name: _Jaina_

Date: _9/10/22_

Tick the circles to show amount of evidence found in writing:

1 No evidence
2 Some evidence
3 Clear evidence

Assessing punctuation

The writing sample demonstrates:	Evidence		
sentence boundaries demarcated with capital letters and appropriate end punctuation.	1	②	3
capital letters used for proper nouns and 'I'.	1	②	3
apostrophes used for contractions and possession.	1	2	③
inverted commas and internal punctuation used to correctly denote direct speech.	①	② 2¹	3
commas used to separate phrases and clauses, including fronted adverbials.	1	②	3
commas, brackets or dashes used to indicate a parenthesis.	1	2	③
commas, colons and semicolons used to punctuate lists.	1	2	③

Assessing grammar and sentence structure

The writing sample demonstrates:	Evidence		
appropriate vocabulary choices [i.e. formal language], including the use of Standard English.	1	②	3
a range of conjunctions to link clauses and to develop and show relationships between ideas.	1	2	③
relative clauses [including parentheses] to clarify, explain or add ideas.	1	②	3
varied verb forms to make time references, including perfect forms [e.g. she had been].	1	②	3
modal verbs and adverbs to express possibility [e.g. thought he might; was perhaps].	1	②	3
adverbs to comment [e.g. undoubtedly; surprisingly].	1	2	③
passive forms to maintain focus [e.g. the book was accepted].	1	2	③
expanded noun phrases to convey information concisely, and adverbials to add detail.	1	②	3

Key target: _____

Writing task 1: Pupil checklist

Name: _Jaina_

Date: _10/10/22_

Reread what you have written to check that it makes sense. Tick the circle if you have correctly used the punctuation or grammar feature in your writing.

Punctuation

- (✓) I have used capital letters at the beginning of sentences, and full stops, question marks or exclamation marks at the end of sentences.
- (✓) I have used capital letters for proper nouns and 'I'.
- (✓) I have used apostrophes in contractions and for possession.
- (✓) I have used inverted commas and other punctuation in direct speech.
- (✓) I have used commas to separate phrases and clauses, including fronted adverbials.
- (✓) I have used commas, brackets or dashes to indicate parenthesis in a sentence.
- (✓) I have used colons, semicolons and commas correctly in a list.

Grammar and sentences

- (✓) I have written in Standard English and used formal vocabulary choices.
- (✓) I have used a range of conjunctions to link clauses and develop ideas.
- (✓) I have used relative clauses to clarify, explain or add ideas.
- (✓) I have used different verb forms to make time references, including perfect forms (e.g. she had been).
- (✓) I have used modal verbs and adverbs to suggest possibilities (e.g. might, perhaps).
- (✓) I have used adverbs to comment (e.g. undoubtedly; surprisingly).
- (✓) I have used adverbials to add detail, and expanded noun phrases to give precise information.
- (✓) I have used the passive voice (e.g. it was accepted).
- (✓) I have used varied sentence openings and types of sentence.
- (✓) I have used pronouns rather than repeating nouns.

Teacher feedback

Jaina You have done well but you need to fill in, I know what your capable of!

My key target: _To write more_

Lesson 11 Structures of informal speech

Focus recognising structures typical of informal speech

Key terms formal, informal, question tag, contraction, exclamation, question

Focus text Mum was on the phone to her friend Mandy.
"Hi, Mandy. That you? Yes, we're fine. Have you heard about Beth? A fracture, apparently. What a shock! You only saw her the other day, didn't you? Hope she's OK."

TEACH

Show the focus text. Read it aloud using appropriate expression. Discuss the situation [e.g. Who is speaking? What about? What might Mandy be saying in reply?]. Discuss whether it is a formal or informal conversation and how we can tell this [informal – it sounds like a chatty conversation because of the greetings and questions; it uses patterns of normal, casual speech].

Explain that it is not only the words used that distinguish informal and formal speech and writing – it is also the sentence structures. For example, in informal speech, the audience [or listener] is often addressed directly through questions and the use of 'you' [e.g. Have you heard about …?]. Informal speech tends to be interactive, inviting a response from the listener. Statements are turned into questions by the use of question tags [e.g. You only saw her the other day, didn't you?].

Point out that informal speech does not always use complete sentences. Sentences are often shortened or incomplete [e.g. That you? A fracture, apparently]. Discuss what is missing from these sentences [e.g. (Is) that you? (She has) a fracture, apparently.]. Explain that the meaning is still clear to the intended audience – the listener.

Explain that we also use these features of informal speech in informal writing [e.g. personal diary; letter to a friend]. Discuss other features used in the focus text that we might use in informal writing [e.g. the use of contractions with apostrophes – 'she's'; the use of exclamations – 'What a shock!'].

EXTEND Discuss how to rework the idea from the focus text into a more formal-sounding letter, using appropriate sentence structures. [Note: Formal writing will be the focus of the next lesson, Lesson 12.]

PRACTISE

Pupil book page 18

APPLY

- The pupils write a story in the first person, deliberately using a chatty, informal style. They use structures from informal speech [e.g. addressing the reader; question tags; contractions; exclamations].
- The pupils write a script for a scene based around family life, replicating structures of informal speech.
- The pupils write a letter using informal sentence structures to achieve a conversational effect.
- The pupils write an advert to appeal to a younger audience, using some structures of informal speech [e.g. questions; question tags; exclamations].

ASSESS

Dictation: I'm going to the gig. Yes, really! Got the tickets and everything. So amazing! Bet you'd go if you could, wouldn't you? Sorry!

Check: The sentence punctuation is correct, including question tags and contractions. [Note: The pupils may decide to end all the sentences with exclamation marks apart from the question. If so, discuss overuse of exclamation marks.]

Pupil book answers

Structures of informal speech

Remember

The sentence patterns used in **informal** speech are different to those used in **formal** speech and writing. Sentences are often incomplete or cut short. The listener is addressed directly. **Question tags**, **exclamations** and **contractions** are often used.

Hi, Mandy. That you? Have you heard about Beth? A fracture, apparently. What a shock! You only saw her the other day, didn't you? Hope she's OK.

Try it

1 Tick which of each pair of sentences uses a sentence structure usually found in **informal** speech. Explain your choice.

A You'll help, won't you? ✓

B I do hope you will be able to help. ☐

A is a question with a question tag.

A There is no way that is possible. ☐

B No way. ✓

B is an incomplete sentence.

A Do you want to hear some news? ✓

B I have some interesting news to share. ☐

A addresses the audience directly.

The pupils may express the reasons in a different way or give other reasons [e.g. they could refer to contractions used in the question-tag example, or to 'no way' being a shorter sentence]. Encourage them to refer to specific structures rather than giving general answers [e.g. it's shorter; it sounds informal].

2 You are sending a message to a friend who is ill. Write a sentence using each of the **informal** sentence structures given below.

incomplete sentence	Heard you're ill.
exclamation	How awful for you!
question tag	You'll be back at school soon, won't you?
contraction	We'll miss you.

These are just examples.

Check that the sentences are punctuated correctly, including the use of capital letters, question marks, exclamation marks, commas with question tags, and apostrophes in contractions.

Sentence practice

Write a short message to a friend using patterns of **informal** speech.

Hi Chloë. How's it going? Coming to my house after school?

18

This is just an example. You could discuss what informal structures have been used.

Check the punctuation [e.g. capital letters; question marks; apostrophes].

Lesson 12 Structures of formal writing

Focus comparing the structures of informal speech with those of formal speech and writing

Key terms formal, informal

Focus text We're having a party on Saturday. Our Ellie's 18th. Buffet, disco, the lot. Quite a do! You will come, won't you?

Mr and Mrs Atkins request the pleasure of your company at a party to celebrate the eighteenth birthday of their daughter Ellie. Formal dress is required.

TEACH

Show the first part of the focus text. Read it aloud and discuss the purpose and audience [e.g. inviting a friend to a party]. Discuss the features that show this is an informal invitation. Refer to both language [e.g. Our Ellie; the lot] and sentence structures [e.g. contractions; shortened or incomplete sentences; exclamations; question tags].

Show the second part of the focus text and read it aloud. Ask the pupils what they notice [e.g. this is a formal invitation to the same party]. Remind the pupils that in formal writing we use different sentence structures as well as different language. For example, sentences are always complete and tend to be longer, using clauses and phrases to add additional information [e.g. in the formal invitation, the invitation and purpose of the party is all given in one sentence].

Explain that in formal writing everything is said carefully and precisely. In formal situations, there are often stock formal phrases not used in everyday speech [e.g. request the pleasure of your company]. Discuss how formal writing also tends to use sentence structures that distance the reader and writer. Explain that building sentences around nouns and using passive forms help to give a more formal tone [e.g. 'Formal dress is required.' sounds more formal than 'Please wear formal dress.']. [Note: Impersonal writing is covered in more detail in the next lesson, Lesson 13.]

EXTEND Discuss the idea of different levels of formality, depending on the purpose and situation [e.g. a legal document would be even more formal than the invitation in the focus text].

PRACTISE

Pupil book page 19

APPLY

- The pupils write invitations to a real or imaginary prestigious event, using formal language and sentence structures.
- The pupils hold formal debates using appropriate language and structures [e.g. let the pupils take on the role of councillors or politicians discussing an important issue].
- The pupils write letters to a real audience about a current issue or concern. They work in pairs to orally rehearse sentences, focusing on achieving a formal tone.

ASSESS

Dictation: Keep your eyes open when you cross the road. <u>Pedestrians should remain vigilant when crossing the road.</u>
Say: Underline the formal version of the sentence.

Pupil book answers

Structures of formal writing

Remember

Formal speech and writing uses language with no **contractions**, **exclamations** or **question tags**. Sentences are always complete and often use **clauses** and **phrases** to add additional information. Sentences are carefully constructed to give a formal tone, sometimes using the **passive voice**.

Mr and Mrs Atkins request the pleasure of your company at a party to celebrate the eighteenth birthday of their daughter Ellie. Formal dress is required.

Try it

1 Complete the **formal** version of each sentence.

Don't smoke in here!

Please refrain from _smoking while on these premises._

That's not what we decided, is it?

There seems to be a misunderstanding _about what was decided._

We've noticed some street lights aren't working.

It has been brought to our attention that _some of the street lighting is not functioning._

2 Rewrite the following as sentences appropriate for **formal** writing.

I'm sorry to tell you, you haven't got the job.

I regret to inform you that your application for the post has been unsuccessful.

Fill in the form and get it signed by a grown-up.

Once all sections have been completed in full, the form should be signed by a responsible adult.

Thanks to your rubbish bus service, I'm always late for school.

The buses on this route are so unreliable that I am frequently late arriving at my destination.

Sentence practice

Write <u>two</u> sentences of a **formal** letter asking for information about disabled access to a town hall.

I am writing to enquire about disabled access to the town hall. I would be very grateful if you could provide me with the necessary information.

19

This activity introduces the pupils to sentence structures and expressions found in formal writing.

The words may not be exactly as shown but the formal tone should be maintained.

There should be no exclamation marks, question tags or contractions.

These are examples of sentences using appropriate language, structures and phrases. No contractions should be used.

Encourage the oral rehearsal of sentences to help the pupils to achieve the appropriate tone.

[Note: References to 'I' are acceptable. Impersonal writing is covered in the next lesson, Lesson 13.]

This is just an example of two sentences that use formal language and formal constructions. Oral rehearsal can be used to develop the sentences.

Lesson 13 Impersonal writing

Focus recognising impersonal writing and using the passive voice to avoid personal references

Key terms formal, **impersonal**, active, passive, personal pronoun

Focus text We have organised a talent show for younger pupils. We hope to raise funds for the new playground equipment. We will give all entrants a certificate.
A talent show has been organised for younger pupils. It will raise funds for the new playground equipment. All entrants will be given a certificate.

TEACH

Show the focus text. Read and compare the two versions. Explain that the same vocabulary is used in both versions but that one sounds more formal than the other. Discuss which sounds the most formal and why [the second version – because it does not include the personal references to 'we'].

Explain that the second version is an example of impersonal writing. Impersonal writing avoids personal references such as names or personal pronouns. There is less sense of *who* is writing. Formal writing is often impersonal [e.g. official documents; science reports]. However, formal and impersonal are not the same. Formal speech and writing can sometimes be personal [e.g. a 'thank you' speech or a letter complaining about bad service may be formal and personal].

Discuss how personal references have been removed in the focus text by using the passive voice [has been organised, will be given]. Remind the pupils that this takes the focus off the person or thing doing the action. The 'do-er' or agent can be omitted so that the personal reference is hidden [e.g. A talent show has been organised (by us).]. Invite the pupils to orally compose other examples [e.g. We will award three prizes./Three prizes will be awarded.].

Explain that in the second sentence, a different technique is used. The impersonal version starts with 'It' rather than 'We' [We hope to/It will]. Explain that we can also use the word 'There' in a similar way [e.g. 'There will be a talent show …' or 'There will be three prizes.'].

EXTEND Discuss other ways of rewording the impersonal sentences [e.g. Certificates will be awarded to all entrants.].

PRACTISE

Pupil book page 20

APPLY

- The pupils use impersonal writing in science [e.g. when writing about investigations]. Encourage the use of the passive voice, hiding the agent [e.g. Three containers were placed …; Water was frozen …].
- The pupils write a news report about a recent event in class or in school, but use an impersonal voice to achieve a formal tone [e.g. The event was held …; There were a number of …].
- Look for examples of impersonal writing in explanations and text books. Encourage the pupils to use the same structures when writing their own formal explanations or information texts.

ASSESS

Dictation: A visit to the library was organised for Monday morning. The librarian showed the children how to use the library. The children were encouraged to select books to read at home.
Say: Underline the sentence *not* written in the passive voice. Rewrite it in the passive voice.
Answer: The children were shown how to use the library (by the librarian).

Pupil book answers

Impersonal writing

Remember

Formal writing is often **impersonal** (although not always). Impersonal writing includes no personal references or personal pronouns – sentences start with 'It' or 'There' rather than 'I' or 'We'. The **passive voice** is often used to 'hide' the person doing the action.

<u>We will give</u> all entrants a certificate.   (active voice – personal)
All entrants <u>will be given</u> a certificate.   (passive voice – impersonal)

Try it

1   Tick the **impersonal** version of each sentence.

Air travel can be expensive.   ✓
Air travel is too expensive for me.   ☐

We will check all passports on arrival.   ☐
All passports will be checked on arrival.   ✓

I would advise you to arrive early at the check-in desk.   ☐
It is advisable to arrive early at the check-in desk.   ✓

The flight in question was delayed for three hours.   ✓
The flight I'm talking about was delayed for three hours.   ☐

> You could discuss the different ways in which the personal reference has been removed [e.g. rewording; using the passive voice and omitting the 'do-er'; starting with 'It'].

2   Rewrite each sentence using the **passive voice** to make it **impersonal**.

We chose Tom to represent the school.   Tom was chosen to represent the school.
I have designed posters for the play.   Posters have been designed for the play.
He added another bulb to the circuit.   Another bulb was added to the circuit.
We will hold the quiz in the hall.   The quiz will be held in the hall.
I grew the tomatoes in the tub.   The tomatoes were grown in the tub.
You can obtain a form from the office.   Forms can be obtained from the office.

> Discuss the change in tone achieved through the use of the passive voice.
>
> If necessary, discuss the changes in verbs and wording required, such as adding auxiliary verb forms [was/were/be/been] and using past participles, including irregular forms [chosen, held, grown].

Sentence practice

Write <u>three</u> sentences about a science experiment, using an **impersonal** style.

A spoonful of the powder was added to the water. The water was stirred for one minute. It was then left for five minutes.

20

This is just an example of sentences using the passive voice or sentences starting with 'It' rather than 'We'/'I'.

You could ask the pupils to write about an experiment relating to their current work in science.

Lesson 14 Verbs: subjunctive form

Focus the use of the subjunctive form in very formal speech and writing

Key terms verb, **subjunctive form**, formal

Focus text If Jay were to apologise, I am sure the matter would be resolved. Therefore, I propose that Jay write a letter of apology to Mr Gill. It is important that this matter be dealt with swiftly.

TEACH

Show the focus text. Read it aloud. Discuss the likely purpose and audience and what situation might have led to it being written. Invite the pupils to comment on the tone of the writing [e.g. it sounds very formal and serious, reflecting the purpose and situation]. Ask the pupils to identify language and structures that help create the formality [e.g. I propose that ...; this matter be dealt with ...].

Explain that the focus text shows a verb form that is only used in very formal or correct speech and writing. It is called the subjunctive form and is only used in particular situations.

Underline the start of the first sentence [If Jay were to apologise]. Ask the pupils if they notice anything unusual about the verb used here [e.g. we would expect 'If Jay <u>was</u>' rather than 'If Jay <u>were</u>', as 'was' shows the usual subject–verb agreement]. Explain that this is the subjunctive form – 'were' is used rather than 'was' in formal sentences beginning 'If I/he/she/it were ...', or in similar sentences referring to wishes or imaginary future situations [e.g. I wish I were ...; Were I/he/she/it to ...].

Underline the start of the main clause in the second sentence [I propose that Jay write ...]. Ask the pupils if they notice anything unusual about a verb used here [e.g. we would expect 'Jay <u>writes</u>' rather than 'Jay <u>write</u>', as –s is the usual verb ending]. Explain that this is another example of the subjunctive form. It comes after phrases such as 'propose/recommend/suggest/demand/insist that'. This form of the verb, without any ending, is used regardless of person [e.g. I/you/she/we/they] or tense.

Underline 'that this matter be dealt with' in the third sentence and discuss this use of the subjunctive. Explain that the subjunctive form 'be' is used after phrases such as 'it is important/essential that ...'].

EXTEND Rewrite the second sentence in the past tense. Explain that the subjunctive form of the verb is always the same, even in the past tense [I proposed that Jay write a letter of apology ...].

PRACTISE

Pupil book page 21

APPLY

- In the role of a fictional head teacher, the pupils write a letter to the parents of a character in a story. They use the subjunctive form, amongst other features of formal language.
- The pupils write imaginative sentences about wishes, using the subjunctive [e.g. I wish I were ...].
- After discussing an important issue, the pupils write a formal report to present a list of recommendations. Use the subjunctive [e.g. I would propose that there be ...].

ASSESS

Dictation: If I <u>were</u> your class representative, I would do my best to represent your views. If it was possible, I would take any concerns to the head teacher.
Say: Underline the subjunctive form in the first sentence. Then change the second sentence so that it uses the subjunctive form.
Answer: 'was' should be changed to 'were'

Pupil book answers

Verbs: subjunctive form

Remember

The **subjunctive form** of a verb is only used in a few special situations in very **formal** speech or writing. The subjunctive form is always the same, regardless of person or tense.

If Jay were to apologise, I am sure the matter would be resolved.
Therefore, I propose that Jay write a letter of apology to Mr Gill.
It is important that this matter be dealt with swiftly.

Try it

1 Underline the **subjunctive form** of the verb in each sentence.

I suggest that Amy try harder to control her temper even when she is provoked.

If the school were awarded the grant, we would use it to build a new library.

I am recommending that Ahmed be given a special award for his efforts.

If I were prime minister, I would make many changes to our laws.

It is essential that the swimming pool remain open to members of the public.

We demand that everyone be treated equally.

2 Complete each sentence with the **subjunctive form**.

The school insists that pupils ___be___ here on time.   (be are)

I wish I ___were___ able to help more people.   (were was)

It is vital that Isabella ___complete___ the quest.   (completes complete)

It is very important that Jack ___attend___ school every day.   (attend attends)

The doctor proposed that he ___avoid___ eating certain foods.   (avoids avoid)

If she ___were___ to have one wish, it would be to visit her family in Australia.   (was were)

Sentence practice

Write **two** sentences about things you wish for, using the **subjunctive form**.

I wish I were faster so I could be an Olympic sprinter. If I were to win the lottery,
I would give a substantial donation to charity.

This activity helps to reinforce the occasions when the subjunctive is used, such as after certain verbs [e.g. suggest/recommend/demand (that) ...] or phrases [e.g. It is essential/important (that) ...], and after 'if'/'as though' to express wishes or something hypothetical.

Reinforce that it is only used in formal situations and a few everyday expressions [e.g. If I were you ...].

You may wish to explain to the pupils that the more usual verb form [e.g. that pupils are here on time] is still correct Standard English, but here the use of the subjunctive is required to make the sentence more formal.

These are just examples of sentences that use the subjunctive to refer to wishes or imaginary future situations. Look for typical structures [e.g. I wish I were ...].

21

Lesson 15 Linking paragraphs

Focus linking ideas across paragraphs using a range of cohesive devices

Key terms paragraph, cohesion, conjunction, adverbial, pronoun, determiner

Focus text Back in the 1960s, travelling into space was an incredible achievement.
However, even at that time, some people believed the cost of space travel could not be justified.

TEACH

Show the first sentence of the focus text. Explain that it is the opening sentence of a paragraph in a text discussing space travel. Read the sentence, identify the main idea and discuss how the rest of the paragraph might develop [e.g. adding detail about space travel in the 1960s; explaining why it was an incredible achievement].

Show the second sentence of the focus text. Explain that this is the opening sentence of the next paragraph in the same text. Read it and discuss what it tells us about the direction of the text and how we can tell [e.g. it is now going to show a contrasting view, which is signalled by the adverb 'However'].

Remind the pupils that it is important to show the reader how the different parts of a text fit together. This is called text cohesion and there are a number of techniques we can use to achieve this – for example, we can use linking adverbials [e.g. However], which clearly signal the relationship between ideas.

Use the highlights in the focus text to discuss other devices used to make links across the two paragraphs. Explain that determiners and pronouns can be used to refer back to earlier ideas [e.g. 'at that time' refers back to the time – the 1960s – mentioned in the previous paragraph]. In addition, the repetition of words and phrases helps to create chains of reference across paragraphs [e.g. travelling into space; space travel].

Discuss what the next paragraph might be about and invite the pupils to orally compose an opening sentence using some of these techniques [e.g. Today, space travel is still an incredible achievement.].

EXTEND Discuss similar devices, including conjunctions, to build cohesion *within* paragraphs.

PRACTISE

Pupil book page 22

APPLY

- When they are writing non-fiction texts, encourage the pupils to think carefully about using the opening and closing sentences of paragraphs to make connections [e.g. referring back or forwards].
- When the pupils are writing narratives, discuss how to use links between paragraphs to create suspense [e.g. ending paragraphs by referring forwards – 'But that was just the start of the problem.'].
- Encourage the pupils to also use adverbials, pronouns and subject references *within* paragraphs to achieve cohesion.
- Remind the pupils to reread their writing, checking that the structure is clear to the reader and improving cohesion between paragraphs [e.g. checking determiners, pronouns, adverbials].

ASSESS

Dictation: The question is whether a longer school day would benefit pupils.
Say: Plan a sequence of paragraphs to develop this theme. Write the first sentence for each paragraph, making it clear how the different paragraphs fit together.

Pupil book answers

Linking paragraphs

Remember

It is important to show how **paragraphs** in a text link together. You can use **adverbials** to show the relationships between ideas. You can use **determiners** and **pronouns** to refer back to earlier ideas. Repetition of key words can also help to maintain the focus.

Back in the 1960s, travelling into space was an incredible achievement. (paragraph 1)

However, even at that time, some people believed the cost of space travel could not be justified. (paragraph 2)

Try it

1 Underline the words and phrases that show how each sentence links to a previous **paragraph**.

On the other hand, there were other children who thought homework was a good idea.

After all that excitement, I slept in late the next morning.

Once I was there, I realised he was right.

Despite all these careful preparations, the expedition started badly.

These suggestions will help you to improve your fitness – but now what about diet?

However, not everyone agreed with this decision and some said it was a foolish idea.

2 Plan a piece of writing called 'Should cars be banned from city centres?'. Write the first sentence for each **paragraph**, making it clear how the ideas fit together.

Traffic congestion is clearly a problem in the city centre.

As a result of congestion, city centres often have very high levels of pollution.

However, if we ban cars, everyone will have to rely on public transport.

Consequently, some people say that a ban on cars is unrealistic.

What all this means is that we need to develop other cleaner types of transport.

Sentence practice

On a separate piece of paper, expand and write the text about space travel, or cars in the city centre. Use **paragraphs**, thinking about how to link your ideas across and within them.

22

There may be small variations between the pupils' answers and those shown. The pupils should be looking for other links apart from adverbials [e.g. determiners, pronouns, noun phrases].

You may wish to discuss what the pupils can tell about the previous paragraph from the given sentence.

The pupils should use their first sentences to show the links between the paragraphs. Look for the use of other devices as well as adverbials, such as the repetition of key words [e.g. traffic; pollution; public transport] and the use of linking pronouns or determiners [e.g. this; this pollution].

Look for the linking of ideas across paragraphs using devices discussed in the lesson.

Look for similar devices being used within paragraphs to develop the main theme, plus the use of conjunctions.

Lesson 16 **Ellipsis**

Focus using the technique of ellipsis to avoid repetition and aid cohesion

Key terms **ellipsis**, punctuation mark

Focus text Have you ever wanted to fly? Well, now you can (fly).
With a Merlin Magic Carpet, you can fly whenever you want to fly.
You can take off and you can land at your chosen destination just moments later.

TEACH

Show the focus text and read it aloud. Discuss what type of text it is [e.g. an advertisement for a new product – the Merlin Magic Carpet]. Ask: Does it sound appealing?

Discuss why the word 'fly' has been deleted in the second sentence [e.g. to avoid repetition; because it sounds better and the sentence still makes sense without it]. Explain that we can omit the word 'fly' because it is expected and predictable. We know 'you can' means 'you can fly' because of what has gone before it, so we do not need to repeat the word.

Explain that this technique is called ellipsis. It means cutting out unnecessary repetition of words or repeated references to the same thing and is a useful way of improving or tightening up our writing.

Read the next sentence of the focus text and discuss which word or phrase could be omitted ['fly' or 'to fly' from the end of the sentence]. Cross out 'to fly' and read the new version of the sentence. Discuss with the pupils how it now sounds better and the meaning is still clear – the reader can tell that it means 'to fly'.

Do the same with the last sentence. This time, discuss how the repeated 'you can' could be omitted. Read the new version of the sentence to show that it sounds better.

The pupils may already be familiar with the term 'ellipsis' being used for the punctuation mark […], as these ellipses are often found in stories even for very young children. Explain that the punctuation mark is often a visual sign that something has been omitted [e.g. that some words have been missed out], or is used to encourage the reader to predict what will happen next. [Note: Using the punctuation mark to achieve different effects is covered in Lesson 26.]

EXTEND Discuss the importance of ensuring that the meaning is still clear when we omit words, so that there is no ambiguity.

PRACTISE

Pupil book page 23

APPLY

- Encourage the pupils to use oral rehearsal to help tighten up sentences before writing them.
- Discuss how many words can be omitted from a sentence without changing the meaning.
- When they are editing writing, remind the pupils to check for repetition of unnecessary words.

ASSESS

Dictation: He went for a walk because he wanted to ~~go for a walk~~. He walked down Ivy Road and then ~~he walked~~ up Lime Street. "Where are you going?" asked his friend Joe. "~~I'm going~~ for a walk," he replied.
Say: Edit the full version of the text, crossing out any words that are not necessary.
Check: The sentence punctuation is correct, including the direct speech. You could also mention the change to a capital 'F' needed in the edited direct speech.

Pupil book answers

Ellipsis

Remember

You can often improve your writing by avoiding unnecessary repetition of words. Sometimes you can miss out a word or phrase because it is expected or predictable and the meaning is quite clear without it. Omitting words in this way is called **ellipsis**.

Have you ever wanted to fly? Well, now you can ~~fly~~.

With a Merlin Magic Carpet, you can fly whenever you want to ~~fly~~.

Try it

1 Cross out the word or phrase in each sentence that could be missed out using **ellipsis**.

They looked in the garage and then ~~they looked~~ in the shed.

I don't think it will snow today but it might ~~snow today~~.

He waved to Lucy and ~~he~~ watched her walk away.

Archie was playing outside and I was watching him ~~play outside~~.

She opened the cupboard and placed the biscuit tin inside ~~the cupboard~~.

One of the robbers distracted the shop owner while the other ~~robber~~ stole the money.

Discuss how the sentences are improved by deleting these words.

2 Rewrite each sentence using **ellipsis** to avoid repeating a word or phrase.

Michael is cooking dinner and I am helping him cook dinner.

Michael is cooking dinner and I am helping him.

She grabbed the telescope and then she ran outside.

She grabbed the telescope and then ran outside.

He started to write it all down, but then he gave up writing it down.

He started to write it all down, but then gave up.

Again, discuss the effect of omitting these words.

Sentence practice

Write <u>two</u> versions of the same sentence to show how **ellipsis** can help to avoid repetition.

I don't think I will go but I might go.

I don't think I will go but I might.

23

This is just an example of two sentences that show understanding of the idea of ellipsis. If necessary, encourage the pupils to use a sentence from the page as a model to help them compose their own example.

Lesson 17 Semicolons between clauses

Focus using a semicolon to separate main clauses

Key terms main clause, semicolon, comma, conjunction, punctuation

Focus text Spectators were flooding into the stadium, the excitement was mounting.
The athletes crouched in their starting positions the crowd fell silent.

TEACH

Show the first sentence of the focus text and read it aloud. Discuss whether the sentence is punctuated correctly [no]. Encourage the pupils to explain why a comma cannot be used here [because each part of the sentence is a main clause and makes sense independently]. Emphasise that a comma cannot be used between two main clauses.

Explain that we *could* add a full stop and capital letter and write the sentence as two separate sentences. However, as there is a close link between the two pieces of information, we might prefer to put them in one sentence to show this continuation of an idea. We could do this using a conjunction [e.g. Spectators were flooding into the stadium <u>and</u> the excitement was mounting.].

Explain that another way of doing this is to use a different punctuation mark: a semicolon, which is stronger than a comma. We can put two main clauses together in a sentence and use a semicolon to mark the boundary between them. Emphasise that we only do this when the two clauses are closely linked. Add the semicolon in place of the comma and read the sentence aloud. Discuss the effect – how it links the two ideas and makes the second idea a continuation of the first.

Show the second sentence and read it aloud. Again, there are two main clauses describing events that are closely linked. They could be joined using 'and' or a semicolon. Ask the pupils to identify where the semicolon should be added to separate the two clauses [after 'positions']. Add the semicolon and read out the sentence. Again, discuss the effect – how it closely links the two events.

EXTEND Invite the pupils to find examples in books of sentences with semicolons, and discuss why a semicolon has been used rather than a conjunction or separate sentences.

PRACTISE

Pupil book page 24

APPLY

- Use the sentences from the focus text as models for the pupils as they use semicolons to write about an exciting event.
- When they are writing a non-fiction text, challenge the pupils to find an opportunity to use a semicolon.
- When the pupils are writing stories and non-fiction texts, encourage them to orally rehearse sentences, considering whether to use full stops, conjunctions or semicolons between the main clauses.
- When they are editing and proofreading their writing, remind the pupils to check that commas are not used between main clauses. If they are, discuss whether a semicolon might be better than a full stop.

ASSESS

Dictation: Some people only seem to focus on the problems with the town centre; in fact, there have been many improvements. The new flower beds, for example, are a welcome addition.
Say: Use one semicolon between two of the main clauses in this passage.
Check: Punctuation is correct, including the use of commas around 'for example'. [Note: The semicolon could also be placed between 'improvements' and 'the new flower beds'.]

Pupil book answers

Semicolons between clauses

Remember

A **semicolon** can be used to separate two **main clauses** in a sentence if they are closely linked in meaning. Semicolons are 'stronger' than commas, which <u>cannot</u> be used to separate main clauses.

Spectators were flooding into the stadium; the excitement was mounting. The athletes crouched in their starting positions; the crowd fell silent.

Try it

1 Insert a **semicolon** between the two **main clauses** in each sentence.

The sun was out; the sky was blue.

It was a cold February morning; a thick layer of frost coated the footpath.

Sanjay was one of the oldest in the class; Shay was one of the youngest.

The two sisters had been apart for a long time; they had much to talk about.

Plenty of his friends had already signed up; William wanted to join them.

On the one hand, a parachute jump would be a thrilling experience; on the other, I don't really like heights.

2 Rewrite each line as necessary, using a **semicolon** between the two **main clauses**.

The man set off down the road. Thomas and Grace followed him.

The man set off down the road; Thomas and Grace followed him.

Robbie enjoys playing chess. His sister Tasha, on the other hand, hates playing board games.

Robbie enjoys playing chess; his sister Tasha, on the other hand, hates playing board games.

On the outside, Max was calm but on the inside, he was fuming.

On the outside, Max was calm; on the inside, he was fuming.

Children should live without fear and they should live without hunger.

Children should live without fear; they should live without hunger.

Sentence practice

Add a **semicolon** and complete the sentence with another **main clause**.

I love mint choc chip ice cream; my brother Louis prefers chocolate ripple.

Remind the pupils that on both sides of the semicolon there should be clauses that make sense independently.

You could discuss how the two ideas are closely linked [i.e. the second idea continues or contrasts with the first], and/or the effect of using a semicolon rather than a full stop or a conjunction [e.g. and; but] to separate the clauses.

The pupils could also use some of these sentences as models to help them construct sentences of their own.

Check that no capital letter is added after the semicolon unless for a proper noun.

In the last two sentences, you may need to remind the pupils to use a semicolon *in place of* the conjunction.

This is just an example of a suitable linked main clause. Check that there is an independent main clause after the semicolon. Check that no capital letter is used after the semicolon unless for a proper noun.

Lesson 18 Colons between clauses

> Focus using a colon to separate main clauses
>
> Key terms main clause, colon, semicolon, punctuation
>
> Focus text The mill workers' demands were clear: they wanted better working conditions.
> Current working conditions were inhumane: some workers were dying.

TEACH

Show the focus text. Explain that it is about a historical dispute between mill workers and mill owners. Read it aloud. Discuss the meaning of 'inhumane' and what it tells us about the dispute.

Discuss the first sentence. Explain that it is made up of two main clauses – both parts of the sentence make sense independently. Ask the pupils to name the punctuation mark used between the two clauses [colon]. The pupils should be familiar with using a colon to introduce a list. Explain that a colon can also be used to separate two main clauses in a sentence – as can a semicolon, but with an important difference.

Explain that in this sentence the colon is used to introduce another clause that expands on something already mentioned in the first clause. The first clause introduces the idea of the workers' demands and the second clause tells us what the demands are.

Invite the pupils to orally compose other sentences on the same theme, following the same model [e.g. The decision was made: there would be a strike.].

Discuss the second sentence. Again, a colon is used to separate two main clauses within a single sentence. Explain that a colon is used rather than a semicolon when the second clause explains, illustrates or gives a reason for the first [e.g. here the second clause explains or illustrates *why* working conditions were inhumane]. If we wanted to use a conjunction to join these two clauses, we could use 'because', but the colon makes the sentence more powerful.

Invite the pupils to orally compose alternative endings for the sentence [e.g. ... every day there were terrible accidents.].

EXTEND Discuss other uses of a colon [e.g. to introduce a quotation or example].

PRACTISE

Pupil book page 25

APPLY

- Invite the pupils to look for different uses of colons in different types of texts [e.g. introducing quotations in an autobiography; giving examples in a text book; separating main clauses in a report].
- Encourage the pupils to use these examples as models to help them use colons in their own writing.
- When writing discussion texts, the pupils construct sentences using colons. They use the first clause to introduce an idea and the second to expand or explain it [e.g. There is one very important problem: ...].

ASSESS

Dictation: Andrew had concerns before they set off: the weather seemed to be closing in. However, the group were determined to reach the summit. Andrew insisted on one rule: they must stay in radio contact at all times.

Say: Use a colon between main clauses twice when punctuating this text.

Pupil book answers

Colons between clauses

Remember

A **colon** can be used to separate two **main clauses** in a sentence if the second clause explains or expands on the first.

The mill workers' demands were clear: they wanted better working conditions.
Current working conditions were inhumane: some workers were dying.

Try it

1 Insert a **colon** in the correct place in each sentence.

Maya should definitely take charge of the money: she is so good with figures.

The family have reached a decision: they will go to Spain.

With all sports, the message is the same: practice makes perfect.

At that moment, we realised the truth: everything he had told us was a lie.

The pilot explained why the flight was delayed: there was a problem with the engine.

Cody couldn't wait to tell his friends: he knew they would be excited.

2 Complete each sentence by adding a **colon** and another **main clause**.

Geeta was an excellent student : she worked hard and always listened.

The book club have made their choice : they will read Treasure Island next.

The weather is very changeable here : some days are fine and others are wet.

Stepping outside, he felt a sudden shiver : it was well below zero out there.

Rowan had always liked Reece : he made everyone laugh.

Sentence practice

Write a sentence about a decision you have made, using <u>two</u> **main clauses** and a **colon**.

After much discussion, we have decided on a suitable pet: we will be getting a hamster.

Remind the pupils that on both sides of the colon there should be clauses that make sense independently.

You could discuss how the two ideas are specifically linked [i.e. the second idea explains or expands the first], and how this differs from using a semicolon to separate the clauses.

These are just examples. Compare the pupils' answers, discussing how the added clause must expand or explain the idea in the first clause.

Check that the pupils have added a colon and a main clause starting with a lower-case letter [unless for a proper noun] and ending with a full stop.

25

This is just an example of a sentence with two main clauses separated by a colon. The second clause should expand or explain the idea introduced in the first clause [e.g. the first clause tells us that a decision has been made and the second clause tells us what it is].

Check that the sentence is punctuated correctly.

Lesson 19 Dashes between clauses

> Focus using a single dash to separate main clauses
>
> Key terms punctuation mark, main clause, dash, formal, informal, semicolon, colon
>
> Focus text Fear gripped Leila – she did not dare move.
> She heard a cry – actually, it was more of a sob.
> She shouted, listening for an answer – nothing came.

TEACH

Show the focus text. Read the sentences aloud. Discuss what effect the writer is trying to achieve and how the structure of the sentences helps to achieve this [e.g. the use of short clauses builds tension and uncertainty].

Look at the first two sentences. Ask the pupils to name the punctuation mark used between the clauses [dash]. Remind the pupils that two dashes can be used to mark a parenthesis in a sentence. Point out that here there is just one dash. It is used to separate two main clauses in a sentence rather than having two separate sentences. Discuss why the clauses might belong in the same sentence [e.g. there is a link; the second clause follows directly from the first; the second clarifies the first].

Explain that a single dash can be used as an alternative to a colon or semicolon to separate two main clauses within a sentence. While colons and semicolons tend to be used in more formal writing, dashes are often used in informal writing and in stories. Invite the pupils to orally compose some more sentences using a dash [e.g. She saw a light – it was just a flicker.].

Explain that dashes are sometimes used for effect [e.g. when a second clause contains something surprising]. Discuss why a dash is used in the third sentence [e.g. to emphasise that there was no answer]. In this sentence, discuss and compare the use of a comma, separating a main clause and a subordinate clause, with that of a dash, which can be used to separate a main clause added to the end of the sentence.

EXTEND Explain that the dash has many uses and that the pupils will see it used to add words and phrases, as well as clauses, to sentences.

PRACTISE

Pupil book page 26

APPLY

- When writing stories, the pupils construct sentences using a dash to add something surprising to the end of a sentence. Remind the pupils not to overuse the dash, or it will lose its effect.
- In informal letters and diaries, the pupils use dashes to add comments about events to the end of a sentence.
- The pupils write information texts for a younger audience and construct sentences using a dash to add a surprising detail or fact to a sentence.
- Together, look at the different ways dashes are used in texts. Encourage the pupils to collect examples and use them as models for their own writing.

ASSESS

Dictation: He heard the men talking – they were talking about him. There was no time to lose. He picked up the walking stick – it was the only weapon he could find.
Say: Use a dash between main clauses twice in this passage.

Pupil book answers

Dashes between clauses

Remember

A single **dash** can be used to separate two **main clauses** in a sentence. Dashes tend to be used more in **informal** writing or in stories – especially for adding something surprising.

Fear gripped Leila – she did not dare move.
She heard a cry – actually, it was more of a sob.

Try it

1 Insert a **dash** in the correct place in each sentence below.

Rhys had done his best – he could do no more.

No-one knows what happened – they simply disappeared.

Suddenly, a hole appeared in the wall – there was just a small circle of light.

Blue whales are the largest living creatures on Earth – they can weigh up to 150 tonnes.

She groped around on top of the wardrobe – there was nothing there but dust.

Sport taught me to play fair – a lesson that has stayed with me throughout my life.

2 Add a **dash** and another **main clause** to complete each sentence.

The man was clearly very angry – his face was bright red.

We heard a siren in the distance – help was on the way.

Never play with fireworks – they can be fatal.

They never thought it would be a problem – they were wrong.

As he dug, there was a clank of metal – something was buried there.

They heard a shout from across the bay – it was a cry for help.

Sentence practice

Write a sentence about something surprising, using <u>two</u> **main clauses** and a **dash**.

The mysterious man turned round – it was my neighbour Jack!

26

If necessary, remind the pupils that the clauses before and after the dash should both make sense independently.

These are just examples. Compare how the pupils have chosen to complete the sentences. Discuss how the two clauses link together [e.g. the second clause elaborates on the first or introduces something surprising].

Check that the pupils have added a main clause after the dash, as instructed. It should start with a lower-case letter [unless for a proper noun] and end with a full stop.

This is just an example. The sentence should have two main clauses and be correctly punctuated. The use of an exclamation mark is optional in this sentence – it is used here to show surprise.

Lesson 20 **Hyphens**

Focus understanding how hyphens can be used to avoid ambiguity

Key terms **hyphen**, ambiguity, punctuation, prefix

Focus text Katie is my fun loving sister.
Katie is my fun-loving sister.

Dad teaches seven year-old children.
Dad teaches seven-year-old children.

Mum's going to recover the old chair.
Mum's going to re-cover the old chair.

TEACH

Show the first pair of sentences in the focus text. Ask the pupils to name the punctuation mark used in the second sentence [hyphen]. Explain that a hyphen is used between *words*. It joins two or more words together and shows that these words should be read together. Read the two sentences aloud so the pupils can hear the effect of the hyphen.

Invite the pupils to explain the different meanings of the two sentences – is Katie [no hyphen] fun and loving, or does she [with the hyphen] love to have fun? Point out that this shows why hyphens are important: they can help to make the meaning clear. Explain that if Katie were fun and loving we would use a comma between the two adjectives, rather than a hyphen, to avoid ambiguity.

Show the second pair of sentences. Ask the pupils to read the sentences and then to explain the different meanings – does Dad teach seven children who are a year old [not very likely] or does he teach children who are seven years old? Point out here *two* hyphens are needed to make the meaning clear.

Show the last example. Ask the pupils to read the sentences and then explain the different meanings – is Mum going to get the chair back from somewhere or is she going to put a new cover on it? Explain that here the hyphen is used with a prefix [re–] in order to distinguish it from another word. Discuss other examples where verbs starting with 're–' could be confusing [e.g. resign/re-sign].

EXTEND Discuss different uses of hyphens, such as compound adjectives [e.g. free-range], compound verbs [e.g. double-click] and numbers [e.g. fifty-two].

PRACTISE

Pupil book page 27

APPLY

- Encourage the pupils to look for the use of hyphens in other subjects [e.g. in maths – 'two-digit numbers', 'three-quarters'; in geography – 'non-European'; in design and technology – 'cross-section'].
- The pupils write advertisements [e.g. for a hotel or theme park], including some adjectives that require hyphens [e.g. child-friendly; fun-filled].
- The pupils write character descriptions including adjectives that require hyphens [e.g. golden-haired; kind-hearted].
- The pupils write amusing headlines to illustrate the need for hyphens [e.g. MPs demand a recount].

ASSESS

Dictation: Here are today's headlines: Man finds twenty one-pound coins; Man-eating shark spotted in ocean; Bargain-hunters camp outside department store.

Say: Write these headlines, choosing the most likely meanings and using hyphens to avoid ambiguity.

Pupil book answers

Hyphens

Remember

A **hyphen** is sometimes used to join words together. It shows that those words should be read together to understand their meaning. Hyphens are used in this way to avoid ambiguity or misunderstanding.

Katie is my fun loving sister.

Dad teaches seven year-old children.

Mum's going to recover the old chair.

Katie is my fun-loving sister.

Dad teaches seven-year-old children.

Mum's going to re-cover the old chair.

Try it

1   Explain the meaning of these phrases, with and without the **hyphen**.

hyphen	my short-sighted cousin	a cousin with poor sight
no hyphen	my short sighted cousin	a cousin who is short and can see
hyphen	plant-eating dinosaurs	dinosaurs that eat plants
no hyphen	plant eating dinosaurs	a plant is eating dinosaurs
hyphen	re-serve a meal	to serve a meal again
no hyphen	reserve a meal	to order a meal

> Answers should show understanding of the different meanings created.

2   Rewrite these sentences using **hyphens** to avoid ambiguity.

I demand a recount of the votes.	I demand a re-count of the votes.
Joe was a quick thinking child.	Joe was a quick-thinking child.
Jet was a green eyed cat.	Jet was a green-eyed cat.
We invited thirty nine year old boys.	We invited thirty nine-year-old boys.
I liked the two seater cars best.	I liked the two-seater cars best.
Try our three course meals.	Try our three-course meals.

> You could discuss the possible ambiguity in the sentence without the hyphen.

Sentence practice

Write <u>two</u> sentences to illustrate why a **hyphen** is needed when adding the **prefix** re– to the word 'signed'.

The manager of the club re-signed his contract.

The manager of the club resigned.

27

> These are just examples of possible sentences showing the different meanings of 'resigned' and 're-signed'.

Revision 2 answers

Focus: modal verbs

The pupils may use different modal verbs, as long as they make sense in the context.

Discuss how different modal verbs indicate different degrees of possibility.

Focus: pronouns

Remind the pupils that pronouns stand in place of a noun [e.g. they = the boys].

Focus: determiners

These are just examples. Check that the words are used as determiners [i.e. before a noun or noun phrase]. This is particularly important with words that can also be used as pronouns [e.g. his; some].

Focus: distinguishing prepositions and conjunctions

Remind the pupils that 'since' is a preposition when it starts a phrase [with no verb] and a conjunction when it starts a clause [with a verb]. Remind them to look at what comes after the word 'since'.

These two pages revise grammatical terms and word classes that have been introduced in previous books. The pupils should now be familiar with the terms and how they function in sentences.

The focus of each activity is given to help identify areas that need reinforcement.

Revision 2

1 Rewrite each sentence with a different **modal verb**.

It might be good news.   It will be good news.

The aeroplane can land at any time.   The aeroplane could land at any time.

I will save you a seat.   I may save you a seat.

2 Underline all the **pronouns** in these sentences.

The boys told <u>me</u> <u>they</u> were going to treat <u>themselves</u> to an ice cream.

Did <u>you</u> see <u>someone</u> take those flowers and put <u>them</u> in a vase?

<u>I</u> found some photos of Dad when <u>he</u> was a baby – let <u>me</u> show <u>you</u> <u>them</u>.

3 Write <u>four</u> sentences, using each pair of words in brackets as **determiners**.

The dog wants those biscuits.   (the those)

You need six players to make a team.   (a six)

Most metals are silver in colour but some metals are gold.   (most some)

I know that several people voted for his idea.   (several his)

4 Write whether the word 'since' is used as a **subordinating conjunction** or a **preposition**. Write 'conjunction' or 'preposition'.

A lot has happened **since** we last met.   conjunction

We have been here **since** last Tuesday.   preposition

Since I was seven, I have not missed a day of school.   conjunction

Since the start of the month, it has rained every day.   preposition

5 Rewrite this sentence with a different **possessive pronoun**.

She knew it was his but she took it anyway.

She knew it was ours but she took it anyway.

28

Focus: possessive pronouns

The pupils can use any possessive pronoun that makes sense in the sentence. The activity checks their knowledge and understanding of the term.

6 Complete each sentence using the **determiner 'a' or 'an'**.

After attending _an_ appointment, _an_ elderly lady waited for _a_ taxi for _an_ hour and _a_ half.

_An_ off-duty police officer saw _an_ accident and called _an_ ambulance immediately.

_A_ guide told us about _a_ unique opportunity to see _an_ island from _a_ hot-air balloon.

7 Write <u>four</u> sentences about a farmer. Choose a different **subordinating conjunction** from the box to use in each sentence.

> before   while   once   unless

The farmer ploughed the field before he planted the turnips.

While watering his crops, the farmer avoided the angry bull.

Once the crops are gathered in, the farmer will have a rest.

The farmer will not be able to feed the animals unless his crops grow well.

8 Underline the **relative pronoun** in the sentence below.

I am sure he is the man <u>who</u> sold us the car.

9 Rewrite each sentence with a different **preposition**.

Charlie stood beneath the sycamore tree.   Charlie stood by the sycamore tree.

Alice sits with Jasmine.   Alice sits behind Jasmine.

Our homework is due in on Friday.   Our homework is due in before Friday.

There will be cakes for tea.   There will be cakes after tea.

10 Complete each sentence with an **adverb** to make the event seem more certain.

I will _definitely_ be there by six o'clock.

She is _surely_ going to make the team this time.

Focus: determiners – using 'a'/'an' correctly

If necessary, explain that 'hour' starts with a vowel *sound* even though it begins with a consonant; 'unique' starts with a consonant *sound* even though it begins with a vowel.

Words added at the start of a sentence should begin with a capital letter.

Focus: subordinating conjunctions

These are just examples. Check that the words are used as conjunctions rather than prepositions [e.g. before] or adverbs [e.g. once].

The sentences should be correctly punctuated. If the sentence starts with the conjunction, there should be a comma after the subordinate clause.

Focus: relative pronouns

Focus: prepositions

These are just examples. Compare the pupils' answers.

Focus: adverbs indicating degrees of possibility

The pupils may use a different adverb [e.g. certainly; clearly] but it must make the event seem more certain.

Writing task 2: Analysis sheet

Tick the circles to show amount
of evidence found in writing:
1 No evidence
2 Some evidence
3 Clear evidence ③✓

Pupil name: _____

Date: _____

Assessing punctuation

The writing sample demonstrates:	Evidence		
sentence boundaries demarcated with appropriate end punctuation and capital letters used where necessary.	①	②	③
apostrophes used for contractions and possession.	①	②	③
inverted commas and internal punctuation used to correctly denote direct speech.	①	②	③
commas, brackets or dashes used to indicate a parenthesis.	①	②	③
commas, colons, semicolons, hyphens and dashes used correctly.	①	②	③

Assessing grammar and sentence structure

The writing sample demonstrates:	Evidence		
appropriate use of informal and formal language and sentence structures including the use of Standard English, as and when appropriate.	①	②	③
a range of conjunctions to link clauses and to develop and show relationships between ideas.	①	②	③
relative clauses [including parentheses and omitted pronouns] to clarify, explain or add ideas.	①	②	③
varied verb forms to make time references, including progressive and perfect forms [e.g. she had been].	①	②	③
modal verbs and adverbs to express possibility [e.g. could/might have; maybe].	①	②	③
passive forms to focus on key ideas [e.g. the car was driven away].	①	②	③
expanded noun phrases to convey information concisely, and adverbials to add detail.	①	②	③
variation in sentence types and sentence openings.	①	②	③
pronouns chosen for clarity and to aid cohesion.	①	②	③

Key target: _____

Writing task 2: Pupil checklist

Name: _____   Date: _____

Reread what you have written to check that it makes sense. Tick the circle if you have correctly used the punctuation or grammar feature in your writing.

Punctuation

◯ I have used capital letters at the beginning of sentences and for proper nouns, and full stops, question marks or exclamation marks at the end of sentences.

◯ I have used capital letters for proper nouns.

◯ I have used apostrophes in contractions and for possession.

◯ I have used inverted commas and other punctuation in direct speech.

◯ I have used commas to separate phrases and clauses and to clarify meaning.

◯ I have used commas, brackets or dashes to indicate parenthesis in a sentence.

◯ I have used colons, semicolons and commas in lists.

◯ I have used colons, semicolons or single dashes between main clauses.

◯ I have used hyphens to avoid ambiguity.

Grammar and sentences

◯ I have written in Standard English when appropriate.

◯ I have used formal or informal language and sentence structures as appropriate.

◯ I have used a range of conjunctions to link clauses and to develop ideas.

◯ I have used relative clauses to clarify, explain or add ideas.

◯ I have used different verb forms to make time references, including progressive and perfect forms (e.g. I was standing, I had seen).

◯ I have used modal verbs and adverbs to suggest possibilities (e.g. could, maybe).

◯ I have used adverbials to add detail, and expanded noun phrases to give precise information.

◯ I have used the passive voice (e.g. The car was driven away.).

◯ I have used varied sentence openings and types of sentence.

◯ I have used pronouns rather than repeating nouns.

Teacher feedback

My key target: _____

Lesson 21 Word classes and homonyms

Focus recognising the word classes of homonyms in different contexts

Key terms word class, **homonym**, noun, verb, adjective, adverb

Focus text What sort of bird can you find in your throat? A swallow!
Why did the cat jump out of the tree? Because it saw the tree bark!
Why was the skeleton embarrassed? Because it made a grave mistake!

TEACH

Read each joke in the focus text: first read the question and then reveal its answer.

Once you have read all the jokes, discuss how the humour has been created using the different meanings of the highlighted words ['swallow' – a bird/to let food pass down your throat; 'bark' – part of a tree/the sound a dog makes; 'grave' – serious/a tomb or burial place].

Explain that words like these, which sound and look the same [i.e. have the same spelling] but have different meanings, are called homonyms. Discuss how we can usually tell the required meaning of a homonym from how it is used in a sentence. However, these jokes rely on creating deliberate ambiguity about the word meanings through the context. As a contrast, invite the pupils to orally compose sentences that make clear both meanings of the homonyms [e.g. A dog began to bark at the rough bark on the tree.].

Explain that a homonym can belong to different word classes, depending on how it is used in a sentence. For example, from the focus text, 'grave' can be a noun [a grave] or an adjective [e.g. a grave mistake]; 'swallow' and 'bark' can be verbs [e.g. I swallow my food. Dogs bark loudly.] or nouns [e.g. a swallow flew; the bark of a tree], and also nouns related to the meaning of the verbs [e.g. the bark of a dog; a swallow or gulp].

Remind the pupils that classifying words as nouns, verbs, adjectives and so on depends on looking at how they are used in a sentence. For example, 'a swallow' is a noun because it comes after a determiner and names something. Discuss the other examples in the focus text ['grave' is used as an adjective because it is used to modify a noun; 'bark' could be a verb *or* a noun – although a tree is unlikely to bark].

EXTEND Discuss words with different pronunciations as well as meanings [e.g. present].

PRACTISE

Pupil book page 32

APPLY

- The pupils collect or write their own jokes that use homonyms ambiguously.
- Using a dictionary, the pupils find some different definitions of words that are homonyms. Encourage them to look at how the word class is given.
- The pupils use homonyms to create humour in headlines, adverts or poetry.
- In other subject areas, encourage the pupils to look for homonyms and/or words that function as verbs and nouns with linked meanings [e.g. to force/the force of gravity; to filter/a filter].

ASSESS

Dictation: Grandma told Holly to listen to the kind words and forget about the rest. Not everyone was mean and greedy.
Say: Write the word class of 'rest' and 'mean'. Then write sentences using these words as verbs.
Answer: noun, adjective; e.g. I must rest for a moment. I didn't mean to do it.

Pupil book answers

Word classes and homonyms

Remember

Homonyms are words that sound the same and are spelt the same but have different meanings. They can belong to different **word classes** (for example, verbs, nouns, adjectives, adverbs). You can tell the word's meaning and its word class from how it is used in the sentence.

The tree bark was rough.	(noun)	The dogs bark loudly.	(verb)
She found an old grave.	(noun)	It was a grave mistake.	(adjective)

Try it

1 Write whether each underlined word is a **noun**, **verb**, **adjective** or **adverb**.

We decided to take the most <u>direct</u> route. — adjective

It was time to <u>free</u> the birds from their cage. — verb

Spaghetti is a <u>type</u> of pasta used in Italian cooking. — noun

I <u>just</u> saw Ivan a minute ago in the playground. — adverb

He <u>left</u> the meeting at six o'clock. — verb

In history we learn about events in the <u>past</u>. — noun

> Remind the pupils to think about how the word is used in the sentence.

2 Write a sentence to include each word from the activity above, using it as in the **word class** shown.

verb	(direct)	Can you direct me to the railway station?
adjective	(free)	There is a free gift with the magazine this week.
verb	(type)	She asked the secretary to type a letter.
adjective	(just)	The judge said it was a just punishment.
adverb	(left)	Go to the end of the street and turn left.
adverb	(past)	The band marched past.

> These are just examples of possible sentences. Any correctly punctuated sentences are acceptable as long as they use the words as directed [e.g. 'left' and 'past' should be adverbs — whereas 'a <u>left</u> turn' = adjective; '<u>past</u> the school' = preposition].

Sentence practice

Write <u>three</u> sentences, using the word 'cross' as a **verb**, a **noun** and then an **adjective**.

verb	Look both ways before you cross the road.
noun	Put a cross in the box.
adjective	My mum was cross this morning.

32

> These are just examples. Any correctly punctuated sentences are acceptable as long as they use the word 'cross' in the three different ways as indicated.

Lesson 22 Nouns with suffixes

Focus revising nouns and noun suffixes; introducing abstract nouns

Key terms noun, determiner, plural, **common noun**, **abstract noun**, suffix

Focus text Should animals have the same rights as humans? Clearly, cruelty to animals is wrong. What about the hunting of animals? Should animals be kept in captivity? Should they be kept for our entertainment? Is the freedom of an animal more important than conservation?

TEACH

Show the focus text. Read it aloud and discuss the issues raised, exploring the meaning of some of the words and concepts [e.g. rights; captivity; conservation].

Ask the pupils to identify the nouns in the focus text. Underline them. As you do this, recap the function and characteristics of nouns. For example, they name things [e.g. animals; humans; cruelty; conservation]; they follow, or could follow, a determiner [e.g. the rights; the hunting; our entertainment; the freedom]; they can be plurals [e.g. animals; rights; humans]. Remind the pupils that not all nouns have a plural form. Some are non-countable [e.g. conservation].

Explain that although all the underlined words are nouns, only a few are common nouns naming people or things [e.g. animals; humans]. Many of the nouns name things that we cannot physically see, touch, hear, taste or smell [e.g. qualities; feelings; ideas; conditions]. These are sometimes called abstract nouns and they are often found in more formal and complex texts [e.g. discussing issues].

Explain that some abstract nouns are formed by adding a suffix to another word. Identify examples in the focus text, discussing the root word and circling the suffixes [e.g. cruel_ty_; captiv_ity_; entertain_ment_; free_dom_; conserv_ation_]. Discuss how sometimes these nouns sound better in sentences than using the root word [e.g. cruelty is wrong/being cruel is wrong].

Explain that sometimes the –ing form of a verb is used as a noun [e.g. the hunting of animals]. The word 'hunting' could have been used as a verb in this sentence [e.g. What about (people) hunting animals?] but using the noun keeps the focus on the animals.

EXTEND Invite the pupils to classify nouns into different types [common/proper nouns, abstract nouns, countable/non-countable nouns – those with/without plurals].

PRACTISE

Pupil book page 33

APPLY

- The pupils write a piece about animal rights using the abstract nouns from the focus text.
- When planning a piece of non-fiction writing together, discuss and record relevant abstract nouns to use in the writing. The pupils practise using them as the subject of sentences [e.g. Transportation is …].
- In stories, the pupils use nouns as well as adjectives to describe feelings [e.g. To his astonishment, …].
- In other subject areas [e.g. science; history], encourage the use of abstract nouns formed by adding suffixes to other words [e.g. absorption, suction; locality].

ASSESS

Dictation: During the speech there was an interruption from a protester. He was protesting about the injustice of poverty. His protest caused much excitement in the hall.
Say: Underline the nouns. Then circle the suffixes used to form any of the nouns.

Pupil book answers

Nouns with suffixes

Remember

Nouns name a variety of things: **common nouns** name things around us; **abstract nouns** name qualities, feelings, ideas or conditions. Many abstract nouns are formed by adding a **suffix** to another word.

cruel**ty**   captiv**ity**   entertain**ment**

free**dom**   conserv**ation**   fair**ness**

Try it

1 Add or replace a **suffix** to make each word into an **abstract noun**. Write the noun.

calm	calmness	weary	weariness
astonish	astonishment	achieve	achievement
aggressive	aggression	desperate	desperation
sincere	sincerity	real	reality
innocent	innocence	relevant	relevance
wise	wisdom	just	justice

2 Write a sentence to include an **abstract noun** formed from each word given in brackets.

There was an awkwardness in the cat's movements.   (awkward)

It did not take much persuasion to make him change his mind.   (persuade)

Her determination to succeed impressed everyone.   (determined)

His curiosity got the better of him and he had to look inside.   (curious)

It is important that older children have some independence.   (independent)

You can check the availability of tickets on the website.   (available)

Sentence practice

Write <u>two</u> sentences, including an **abstract noun** formed from each of the words 'educate' and 'require'.

Education is very important. It is a legal requirement in many countries.

33

The nouns should be spelt correctly. The pupils could use a dictionary to help, if necessary.

You could ask the pupils to orally compose sentences using the nouns, to check their understanding of the words and give extra practice at forming sentences around nouns.

These are just examples of possible sentences using the nouns in an appropriate context.

If the pupils struggle, encourage them to start by trying determiners before the noun [e.g. an awkwardness; the awkwardness; his awkwardness]. Once they have a noun phrase, they can build a sentence around it using oral rehearsal.

The nouns should be spelt correctly.

These are just examples of sentences using the nouns 'education' and 'requirement'.

Lesson 23 **Sentence variation**

Focus using different types of sentence; varying sentence length, order and focus

Key terms question, command, statement, exclamation, clause, active, passive

Focus text Have you ever thought about what it would be like in a world without gravity?
When the correct date appears, press 'OK'.
Nobody moved.
In 2012, the company made its first robotic device, which was instantly a worldwide success.

TEACH

Show the sentences from the focus text one at a time. Read each sentence and discuss what type of text it might be from [e.g. an information text aimed at younger readers; an instruction manual; an adventure story; information about a company]. Discuss what features of the sentence suggest this [e.g. the question to introduce the subject and engage the reader; the command "press 'OK'"].

Explain that the focus text shows a range of different sentences. There are different sentence types [question, command, statement]; different lengths [e.g. one clause; more than one clause] and different sentence openings [verb, conjunction, pronoun, preposition].

Explain that when we write, we should use a range of sentences. This is true of all writing, although the type of text, the purpose and the audience help us choose sentence structures appropriate for a particular piece of writing. For example, we would use a command when writing instructions [e.g. press 'OK']; a question if we wanted to engage or address the reader [e.g. Have you ever thought ...?] or an exclamation to show strong feelings [in informal writing but not in formal writing].

We can vary sentence length, using short sentences for impact [e.g. Nobody moved.] and longer sentences to develop ideas and add detail. [Note: The next lesson, Lesson 24, covers multi-clause sentences.] We can start sentences in different ways [e.g. with an adverb/preposition/conjunction/verb/adjective/noun] and reorder sentences for effect [e.g. moving adverbials –"Press 'OK' when ..."].

Explain that we can also vary the focus of a sentence, and demonstrate changing the last sentence from active to passive so that the focus is on the device, rather than the company [The first robotic device was made in 2012 ...].

EXTEND Investigate sentence structures used in a particular type of text [e.g. a formal report].

PRACTISE

Pupil book page 34

APPLY

- When the pupils are writing, encourage oral rehearsal to try out different versions of sentences.
- Display lists reminding the pupils how sentences can be varied. They then refer to them as they write.
- The pupils write story extracts or advertisements, varying sentence types as much as possible.
- The pupils write factual texts using a variety of sentence types to engage the reader [e.g. questions].
- Encourage the pupils to edit their work, reordering sentences for effect.

ASSESS

Dictation: He was lost. What should he do? Any landmarks were hidden by the thick fog.
Say: Continue the passage using a variety of sentences.
Check: Look for different sentence types, lengths, and openings, as well as any use of the passive voice.

Pupil book answers

Sentence variation

Remember

Good writing uses a range of different sentences. For example, you can vary the length of your sentences. You can also use different types of sentence: **statements**, **questions**, **commands** and **exclamations**. In addition, sentences can be started in different ways or reordered for effect.

What would it be like in a world without gravity?
When the correct date appears, press 'OK'.
Nobody moved.

Try it

1. Rewrite this sentence in a variety of ways, using the instructions given in **bold** below.

   Harry dropped the bottle on the floor.

shorter (more impact)	Harry dropped it.
longer (more detail)	In his hurry to escape from the laboratory, Harry dropped the bottle on the stone floor and it shattered in an explosion of tiny fragments.
add to the start	Unfortunately, Harry dropped the bottle on the floor.
use passive voice	The bottle was dropped on the floor (by Harry).
question	Did Harry drop the bottle (on the floor)?
command	Harry, drop the bottle (on the floor).

2. Write at least <u>four</u> sentences to publicise the event below, using a variety of sentence types and lengths.

   We are having a jumble sale to raise money for charity. We need your items to sell.

   Is your garage full of junk? Is your attic overflowing? Donate your junk to our car boot sale and let us turn it into cash. We are looking for unwanted items that we can sell to raise money for charity. Toys, books, ornaments or clothes will all be gratefully accepted.

Sentence practice

Write a wide variety of sentences, using the word 'fascinating' in each one. Write your sentences on a separate piece of paper.

34

In most cases these are just examples and the exact wording may vary [e.g. the pupils may have expanded or started the sentence in different ways; Harry's name might not be mentioned in the command or as the agent in the passive voice]. Compare the pupils' answers to explore the variety of possible sentences.

All sentences should be correctly punctuated [e.g. commas after fronted adverbials and fronted names, and preceding question tags if used].

These are just examples. Look for use of different types of sentence [e.g. questions; commands], different lengths [e.g. long followed by short], and variety in openers [e.g. not too many starting with 'we'].

Compare the pupils' answers and discuss the variety of sentences used.

Look for different types and lengths of sentence, variety in how they begin, and any use of the passive voice [e.g. This fascinating book was written by ...].

You could reinforce the difference between an exclamation strictly defined, starting with 'What' or 'How' [e.g. How fascinating!], and an exclamatory statement [e.g. That was fascinating!].

Lesson 24 Multi-clause sentences

Focus forming sentences containing more than one subordinate clause

Key terms **single-clause sentence**, **multi-clause sentence**, main clause, subordinate clause, relative clause, co-ordinating conjunction, subordinating conjunction, comma, parenthesis

Focus text Jason could not become king until he had claimed the Golden Fleece, which was guarded by a huge snake. So that he could travel across the ocean, Jason had a boat built, which was called the Argo, and he chose a crew, called the Argonauts, to go with him on his quest.

TEACH

Show the focus text. Read it aloud. Explain that it is a summary of the story 'Jason and the Argonauts'. Ask the pupils if they can then summarise what happened next, or predict what might happen [e.g. adventures; dangers; problems; monsters]. Next, ask them to count the sentences in the focus text [only two]. Discuss how so much information has been included in just two sentences [e.g. through the use of subordinate clauses].

Explain that these sentences are multi-clause sentences – they have more than one clause. We use multi-clause sentences to develop and link a number of ideas together in one sentence. If the focus text was written in single-clause sentences – with just one [main] clause in each – it would sound disjointed [e.g. Jason could not become king. He had to claim the Golden Fleece. It was guarded by a huge snake.].

Explain that a multi-clause sentence can include two or more main clauses, joined by co-ordinating conjunctions, or a main clause and one or more subordinate clauses. Discuss the sentences in the focus text, identifying the main clauses; the subordinate clauses with subordinating conjunctions [e.g. until, so that]; and the relative clauses [including those in parenthesis and with omitted pronouns]. Point out that in multi-clause sentences commas separate the different parts of the sentence to ensure that the reader can follow the meaning [e.g. marking the relative clauses used in parenthesis].

Work with the pupils to construct another multi-clause sentence for the focus text or another story. Try out different constructions to find a way of combining several pieces of information into a coherent sentence [e.g. trying different conjunctions; reordering information].

EXTEND Discuss using embedded relative clauses with omitted pronouns to express ideas succinctly [e.g. Jason, (who is) the hero of the story, ...].

PRACTISE

Pupil book page 35

APPLY

- The pupils write summaries of stories using multi-clause sentences to help express ideas economically.
- Encourage the pupils to orally rehearse multi-clause sentences, combining information in different ways.
- When they are writing, remind the pupils to vary sentence length, as the occasional short, single-clause sentence can be very effective [e.g. to highlight key points in non-fiction texts; for impact in stories].
- The pupils write information texts or news reports using embedded subordinate clauses for economy.

ASSESS

Dictation: He lifted the tin out of the box. He heard a rattling noise. He looked inside. He saw the key.
Say: Rewrite this as one multi-clause sentence.
Answer: e.g. As he lifted the tin out of the box, he heard a rattling noise and when he looked inside, he saw the key.

Pupil book answers

Multi-clause sentences

Remember

A **single-clause sentence** has just one clause – a **main clause**. A **multi-clause sentence** contains two or more clauses, which are linked by **conjunctions** or **relative pronouns**. In a multi-clause sentence you can develop and link together a number of ideas.

Jason could not become king **until** he had claimed the Golden Fleece, which was guarded by a huge snake.

Try it

1 Underline all the **subordinate clauses** in these multi-clause sentences.

Although the museum has only been open a month, it has already attracted many visitors after it was featured on a national television programme.

Of course, I knew that something was wrong when Mum kept piling the spaghetti on to the plate until it started to spill all over the floor.

Long before clocks were invented, people measured time using sundials, which showed the time of day by the movement of shadows.

The two vehicles were travelling at speed when they crashed into the cyclist, who was later taken to hospital.

When the police returned to the scene of the crime, the witness soon found the place where he had seen the stolen painting but it had vanished.

2 Rewrite each set of single-clause sentences as a **multi-clause sentence**.

Leah liked the colour of her new coat. She took it back the next day. It was too big.

Although Leah liked the colour of her new coat, she took it back the next day because it was too big.

The cacao tree is an evergreen tree. It originally came from the Amazonian rainforest. It is now grown throughout the tropical regions of the world.

The cacao tree, an evergreen tree that came originally from the Amazonian rainforest, is now grown throughout the tropical regions of the world.

Sentence practice

Write a **multi-clause sentence** giving several facts about a snake or lizard.

Although it is not poisonous, the python, which lives in Africa and Asia, is one of the longest and most deadly snakes.

35

Check that relative clauses have been underlined.

Additional main clauses should not be underlined [e.g. 'but it had vanished' at the end of the fifth sentence]. Remind the pupils that main clauses are joined by co-ordinating conjunctions [and, but, or].

The pupils may have linked the clauses in different ways. Encourage oral rehearsal of sentences.

Compare the pupils' answers to see how they have worked the information into a coherent sentence.

Commas should be used to separate fronted subordinate clauses or a parenthesis – brackets could also be used for any parenthesis.

This is just an example of a sentence the pupils might write. Encourage oral rehearsal of the sentence before the pupils start writing.

Look for a sentence that combines at least three pieces of information. Check that the sentence is punctuated correctly [e.g. using commas to clearly separate the clauses]. Brackets or dashes could be used for any parenthesis.

Lesson 25 Punctuation to avoid ambiguity

Focus using commas and other punctuation to clarify meaning and avoid ambiguity

Key terms punctuation, comma, ambiguity, semicolon

Focus text At the end of our act, the audience applauded thankfully.
At the end of our act, the audience applauded, thankfully.
The gymnasts, who had practised all week, were brilliant.
The gymnasts who had practised all week were brilliant.
Of course, I hate magicians like you I find them so boring.

TEACH

Show the first two sentences of the focus text. Ask the pupils to spot the difference between them [an extra comma in the second sentence]. Read the sentences aloud and discuss their different meanings [e.g. without the comma, the audience is glad that the act is over; with the comma, the writer is grateful that the audience applauded]. Explain that the comma shows that the adverb is meant to comment on the whole sentence rather than just the verb.

Show the two sentences about the gymnasts. Discuss how the commas are used in the first sentence to show that the relative clause is a parenthesis. In the second sentence, there are no commas so the relative clause is not a parenthesis. Read the sentences aloud. Discuss the different meanings of the two sentences [e.g. with the commas, all the gymnasts had practised all week and were brilliant; without the commas, only those gymnasts who had practised all week were brilliant].

Remind the pupils that punctuation helps the reader to understand what we write. Commas are important because they help make the meaning of a sentence clear. They separate parts of sentences and help to avoid ambiguity, as shown in the focus text.

Show the last sentence of the focus text. Ask the pupils to read the sentence and explain the potential ambiguity [is it 'magicians like you' or 'like you, I find them so boring'?]. Ask the pupils to decide where a comma and semicolon should be placed to separate the different parts of the sentence and make the meaning clear ['Of course, I hate magicians; like you, I find them so boring.' is most likely].

EXTEND Discuss how reordering sentences can also resolve ambiguity [e.g. Thankfully, at the end …].

PRACTISE

Pupil book page 36

APPLY

- Remind the pupils to take care, when using relative clauses, to be sure about whether the information is part of the main sentence [so needs no commas] or an added detail [to be demarcated by commas].
- Encourage the pupils to say and read sentences aloud to help determine where commas are needed.
- Ask the pupils to proofread their own writing, checking that the punctuation, particularly the use of commas, helps to make the meaning clear.

ASSESS

Dictation: The children, who had eaten the cake, were feeling ill. The doctor arrived, happily.
Say: Write the sentences with and without commas, and explain the different meanings.
Answer: e.g. Were all the children ill or only those who ate the cake? Was the doctor happy or the writer?

Pupil book answers

Punctuation to avoid ambiguity

Remember

Punctuation helps the reader to understand what you have written. For example, **commas** separate parts of sentences to make the meaning of a sentence clear — they help to avoid ambiguity.

The gymnasts, who had practised all week, were brilliant. (all of them)

The gymnasts who had practised all week were brilliant. (only those who had practised)

Try it

1 Explain how the **commas** change the meaning in each pair of sentences.

The meals, which were cold, were sent back to the kitchen.
The meals which were cold were sent back to the kitchen.

| commas | All the meals were sent back. |
| no commas | Only the meals that were cold were sent back. |

Olivia, thought Lucy, could be hiding something.
Olivia thought Lucy could be hiding something.

| commas | Lucy thought Olivia could be hiding something. |
| no commas | Olivia thought Lucy could be hiding something. |

The children all behaved, naturally.
The children all behaved naturally.

| comma | Of course the children behaved well. |
| no comma | The children behaved in a natural way. |

2 Rewrite each sentence using a **comma** or commas to make the meaning clear.

Amelia went off eating chocolate.   Amelia went off, eating chocolate.

Tigers which have stripes live alone.   Tigers, which have stripes, live alone.

I hate liars like you.   I hate liars, like you.

He said nothing strangely.   He said nothing, strangely.

Sentence practice

Write <u>two</u> versions of a sentence to show how **commas** change the meaning.

Everyone joined in happily.

Everyone joined in, happily.

36

The answers should explain the meaning of both sentences.

If necessary, encourage the pupils to read the sentences aloud to hear the difference.

You could discuss the possible ambiguities in the sentences and how commas help to make the meaning clear [e.g. all tigers live alone, not just those with stripes].

The pupils may have reordered some of the sentences to clarify the meaning [e.g. Like you, I hate liars.]. This still requires use of a comma and so is a good answer. You may wish to discuss this idea with the pupils.

This is just an example. Encourage the pupils to use other sentences from the lesson, if necessary, as models for writing their own.

Lesson 26 **Punctuation for effect**

Focus   using punctuation for effect [e.g. exclamation mark, dash, ellipsis]

Key terms   punctuation, exclamation mark, dash, ellipsis, inverted commas

Focus text   "The ... the ... there's a monster out there," said Emily, trembling. The clawing outside the door certainly sounded terrifying (but I pretended to be brave).
I approached the door – very slowly. I flung it open. You wouldn't believe it ...
There was Emily's 'monster' – it was a fluffy, white cat!

TEACH

Show the focus text. Read it aloud using expression to match the punctuation. Discuss what effect the writer was trying to achieve [e.g. suspense; surprise].

Explain that as well as using punctuation to make meaning clear, we sometimes choose punctuation for the effect it creates. For example, discuss why an exclamation mark has been used at the end of the focus text [e.g. to emphasise the surprise; to make the final statement humorous]. Ask the pupils to identify other punctuation marks used for effect in the focus text [e.g. ellipses (...); dashes].

Point out that an ellipsis [...] has a number of uses and is often used for effect. For example, in the focus text it is used firstly to show faltering speech [The ... the ... there's] and later to create a dramatic pause [You wouldn't believe it ...], encouraging the reader to guess what comes next.

Discuss how other punctuation marks are used for effect in the focus text. The brackets contain the thoughts of the narrator, so allowing us to see 'inner thoughts' as well as actions. A dash is used firstly to emphasise the words 'very slowly' and then to create a dramatic pause at the end. Explain that the dash is another punctuation mark widely used to create effects.

Circle the use of inverted commas around the word 'monster' in the last sentence. Discuss what this suggests [e.g. that it is not a real monster]. Explain that inverted commas are sometimes used like this to draw our attention to the use of a word or phrase and to make us think about whether it is true.

EXTEND   Discuss how the colon and semicolon are used for effect in more formal texts rather than a dash [e.g. The message is clear: smoking kills.].

PRACTISE

Pupil book page 37

APPLY

- The pupils write the dramatic climax to a story using punctuation for effect [e.g. surprise; tension].
- The pupils write a short dialogue for a story. They use punctuation for effect and to show character [e.g. using ellipses to show pauses or hesitations].
- The pupils write informal texts such as letters and diaries, using punctuation to create a lively effect.
- Encourage the pupils to edit a piece of writing, using punctuation to enhance different effects.

ASSESS

Dictation: At that moment, my dad thought it would be 'cool' to get up and dance. It was so embarrassing – seriously! Well, I had to go and hide. (I couldn't watch, could I?)
Say: Punctuate the text for effect.
Answer: Some variation is allowable [e.g. dashes/brackets].

Pupil book answers

Punctuation for effect

Remember

Punctuation can make your writing more effective. For example, **dashes** can be used to emphasise part of a sentence or create a dramatic pause; **exclamation marks** to indicate humour or surprise; **inverted commas** to draw attention to a word or phrase; and **ellipses** (…) to suggest a pause or a cliff-hanger.

"The … the … there's a monster outside," whimpered Emily.

I approached the door – very slowly. I flung it open.

You wouldn't believe it …

There was Emily's 'monster' – it was a fluffy white cat!

Try it

1   Name each circled **punctuation mark**, and explain why the sentence uses it.

Oh no! The bucket landed on Emma's head!

   exclamation mark   It shows surprise and perhaps humour.

After all, nothing could go wrong now …

     ellipsis   It creates a cliff-hanger.

I tried – but it was no use.

     dash   It emphasises that it was no use.

He said she was just being friendly. She was 'friendly' all right.

   inverted commas   They show it is not quite true.

2   Rewrite each sentence using a **punctuation mark** for effect.

"It's it's impossible," he stammered.	"It's … it's … impossible," he stammered.
I am your friend truly.	I am your friend – truly.
Then everything began to go wrong.	Then everything began to go wrong …
The dragon lay dead on the floor.	The dragon lay – dead – on the floor.
We started with the easy questions.	We started with the 'easy' questions.

Sentence practice

Write <u>three</u> sentences about being trapped in a lift. Use **punctuation** for effect.

I was trapped in a lift with a gorilla! "N … n … nice gorilla," I stammered.

Actually, he didn't look very nice – quite the opposite, in fact.

37

The explanations should refer to the effect in that sentence rather than make general comments [e.g. because there's more to come; because it separates parts of the sentence].

The pupils may choose other ways of punctuating the sentences [e.g. The 'dragon' lay dead on the floor. The dragon lay 'dead' on the floor. The dragon lay dead on the floor!]. Encourage them to use a range of punctuation.

Compare the pupils' answers and the effects created.

This is just an example of how punctuation might be used for effect [e.g. to create humour – as here – or tension].

Check that sentence boundaries are still demarcated correctly.

Lesson 27 Varied verb forms

Focus   using varied verb forms to express a range of time references

Key terms   tense, verb, past tense, present tense, **past progressive**, past perfect, **present progressive**, present perfect

Focus text   Before he left, he looked up at the window one last time. That was when he caught a glimpse of her. She was standing in the window, staring down at him.
He knew at once that he had seen her somewhere before.

TEACH

Show the focus text. Explain that it is taken from a story. Read it aloud. Discuss how a sense of mystery is created about the girl [e.g. through how she is introduced and the reference to having seen her before].

Discuss the use of tense in the focus text [e.g. it is a story so it is in the past tense]. Identify and underline the past tense verbs [e.g. left; looked; caught; was standing]. Explain that although there are two basic tenses, past and present, there are different verb forms within these tenses.

Discuss the past tense verb forms used in the focus text. Ask the pupils to identify an example of the past progressive form [she <u>was standing</u>]. Discuss why it is used here rather than the simple past tense 'she stood' [e.g. because she was already standing there when he looked up]. Ask the pupils to find a verb in the past perfect form [he <u>had seen</u>]. Discuss why this is used rather than 'he saw' [e.g. to refer back to an event that happened earlier].

Explain that the same verb forms can be used in the present tense. Work with the pupils to rewrite the focus text in the present tense [e.g. Before he leaves, he looks up ...; She is standing ...]. Identify and discuss the examples of present progressive and present perfect forms. Identify also the verb that does not change [<u>staring</u> down].

Discuss how we use progressive and perfect verb forms in writing to make different time references clear. Explain that we can also combine the perfect and the progressive – for example, the focus text might continue in the past tense: 'About a week ago, he <u>had been walking</u> ...'.

EXTEND   Discuss how a non-finite verb [e.g. staring] takes its tense from another verb in the sentence.

PRACTISE

Pupil book page 38

APPLY

- The pupils write a story with a flashback or reference to earlier events. They use the perfect form of verbs to show the time relationship between events.
- The pupils write accounts and news reports in the past tense but using some past progressive and past perfect forms.
- The pupils write explanations in the present tense but using different verb forms to show links and cause [e.g. when water is moving; once the rock has been worn away].

ASSESS

Dictation: Sonya <u>has been ice-skating</u> for five years. She hopes that one day she will compete for her country. She started skating with her brother. They (were hoping) to compete together but then he was injured.
Say: Underline any present perfect verb forms and circle any past progressive verb forms.

Pupil book answers

Varied verb forms

Remember

English has two basic tenses: **past** and **present**. However, within these tenses you can use different **verb forms** to make clear time references.

He <u>looked</u> up one last time.   (simple past tense)
He <u>was looking</u> up at the window.   (past progressive)
He <u>had looked</u> up there before.   (past perfect)

Try it

1 The passage below is written in the **present tense**. Circle the <u>two</u> **present perfect** verb forms and underline the <u>two</u> **present progressive** verb forms.

It is Saturday afternoon and we are at the Rossley Stadium. The manager (has chosen) an attacking team and it seems to be working. The United players (have started) brightly. Anderson <u>is looking</u> lively and United <u>are pressing</u> the opposition's goal.

Rewrite the passage above using the past tense. Then circle the <u>two</u> past perfect verb forms and underline the <u>two</u> past progressive verb forms.

It was Saturday afternoon and we were at the Rossley Stadium. The manager (had chosen) an attacking team and it seemed to be working. The United players (had started) brightly. Anderson <u>was looking</u> lively and United <u>were pressing</u> the opposition's goal.

2 Complete each sentence using the **perfect form** of a verb.

The soldiers arrived as soon as <u>the family had hidden in the barn.</u>

We can have a break now because <u>we have completed the task.</u>

We had to pick up all the bins after <u>the wind had blown them over.</u>

Complete each sentence using the progressive form of a verb.

We heard a noise and <u>saw that someone was following us.</u>

Ryan prefers acting but <u>at the moment he is singing in a band.</u>

It was late by now and <u>the street lights were coming on outside.</u>

Sentence practice

Write some sentences to show as many different **forms** of the **verb** 'fly' as you can. Write your sentences on a separate piece of paper.

38

You could discuss why these verb forms are used rather than the simple present tense [e.g. present perfect 'has chosen' shows that the team was chosen earlier but still exists; present progressive 'is looking' shows that Anderson's 'looking lively' is a continuing state].

As above, you could discuss what the verb forms show.

These are just examples – the pupils may use different verbs and ideas, but the use of tense must be maintained within the sentence.

Compare the pupils' answers, discussing how the past and present perfect progressive forms refer to events that happened or began to happen earlier, or events that were or are in progress.

Look for a variety of different present and past tense forms [e.g. Birds fly in the sky. We are flying to Germany. They flew to Bali last week. He had flown before.]. The pupils may also combine the perfect and progressive forms [e.g. The pilot has/had been flying for some time.].

Lesson 28 Changing tense

Focus tense consistency; using more than one tense and handling time shifts

Key terms tense, past tense, present tense, adverbial, modal verb, past perfect

Focus text I always thought time travel was impossible. It was something we only read about in stories. But now, as I sit here in my time pod, I am a believer. In the future, we will all travel through time – and I am going to be the first.

TEACH

Show the focus text and read it aloud. Discuss who the 'writer' might be and what is about to happen to him/her. Discuss the reflections on the past [time travel was impossible], what is happening now [I sit in my time pod] and the predictions about the future [we will all travel through time].

Explain that usually a piece of writing maintains the same tense throughout – past tense or present tense. However, sometimes we might use more than one tense in a text, in a paragraph or even in a sentence. For example, the focus text refers to the past, the present and the future in just a few sentences.

Point out that when we do this it is helpful to use adverbials [e.g. now; In the future] to clearly signal the changes in time reference – otherwise it might look as if we have just mixed up tenses. Invite the pupils to orally construct sentences using two tenses [e.g. Once, going to the moon was impossible, but now ...; Now, I sit and wait but soon ...].

Explain that the English language has no specific future tense. Instead we refer to events in the future in a number of ways: using the modal verb 'will' with a present tense verb [e.g. we <u>will travel</u>], the present progressive 'am/are/is going to' with a verb [e.g. I <u>am going to be</u> late], or the simple present tense [e.g. I <u>leave</u> tomorrow].

Discuss how to rework the focus text in the past tense, using past perfect forms to refer to events that happened earlier [e.g. I had always thought], simple past tense [as I sat there] and 'would' to refer to the future.

EXTEND Compose sentences involving two changes in time [e.g. In the past ... but now ... and maybe in the future ...].

PRACTISE

Pupil book page 39

APPLY

- The pupils write about memories of the school year, reflecting on events and their significance, both now and in the future. They use adverbials to clearly signal shifts in tense [e.g. At the time ... but now ...].
- The pupils write an ending for a story that looks back or looks forward, using changes in tense.
- The pupils write a news report that describes what happened, what the situation is now and what is expected to happen in the future.

ASSESS

Dictation: Humans have always been great explorers, travelling far from their own lands to discover new worlds. Now, much of the Earth has been explored and people are looking beyond it into space. <u>The next great challenge will be to explore other planets.</u>
Say: Underline the sentence that refers to the future.

Pupil book answers

Changing tense

Remember

You usually keep to the same **tense** within a piece of writing. However, sometimes more than one tense is needed, so that you can refer to events in the past, present or future. It is important to clearly signal any changes in tense.

I always thought time travel was impossible. <u>Now</u>, as I sit here in my time pod, I am a believer. <u>In the future</u>, we will all travel through time.

Try it

1 Complete each sentence using the correct **tense**.

The town is now a busy port but back then <u>it was just a small fishing village.</u>

He used to just sing in front of friends but today <u>he fills huge stadiums.</u>

Today, his paintings are priceless but in his lifetime <u>he could not sell them.</u>

Currently, he has three shops but in the future <u>he is going to open more.</u>

2 Write another sentence after each sentence below, about something that happened earlier.

He suddenly remembered where the key was. <u>He had hidden it in the library months ago.</u>

Now it is almost time to announce the winner. <u>Earlier today, we chose three finalists.</u>

Write another sentence after each sentence below. This time, write about something that will happen in the future.

At the moment, solar power is expensive. <u>In the future, it might become more affordable.</u>

I thought the concert was brilliant. <u>I will definitely go to see this band again.</u>

Sentence practice

Write <u>three</u> sentences about computers in the past, the present and the future.

<u>At first, computers were used to do complicated calculations. Today, computers have many uses at home and in the workplace. In the future, computers will do even more tasks.</u>

39

Here the changes in tense are clearly signalled by adverbials [e.g. back then; in his lifetime].

These are just examples but the pupils must use the appropriate tense. The future can be expressed in different ways [e.g. going/ planning to; will/will be], all of which are acceptable.

These are just examples. If the given sentence is in the past tense, the pupils should use the past perfect form in the second sentence. When the sentence is in the present tense, they could use the simple past tense or the present perfect [e.g. we have chosen three finalists]. The change in tense could be signalled by an adverbial or time reference.

These are just examples of sentences referring to future events. The pupils may use different verb forms. The tense change could be signalled by a time adverbial.

This is an example of three sentences referring to the past, present and future through the use of adverbials and appropriate tense choices. The sentences could be developed further [e.g. through additional clauses].

The sentences should be correctly punctuated.

Lesson 29 Standard English: confusing words

Focus recognising confusing words [e.g. lend/borrow; beat/win; less/fewer; learn/teach]

Key terms Standard English, antonym, synonym, formal, informal

Focus text "Hiya. I want to lend a book about grammar," said the young girl.
"You would like to *borrow* a book about grammar," sniffed the librarian, coldly.
"Yeah. Miss Li is learning us about it at school," said the girl.
"Miss Li is *teaching* you, is she?" said the librarian. "Well, we have the Complete Grammar Guide."
"Wow! That's a big book. Do you have one with less pages?"

TEACH

Show the focus text. Read it aloud using suitable expression. Discuss the humour in the exchange between two contrasting characters [e.g. the girl with her informal language and the more formal, precise librarian]. Discuss why the librarian repeats and corrects what the girl says – ask the pupils why the words 'borrow' and 'teaching' are in italics [to emphasise the correct choice of word].

In Standard English, it is important to use the correct word. Explain that the verbs 'lend'/'borrow' and 'teach'/'learn' are often confused. Discuss these words ['teach' and 'learn' are opposites or antonyms: 'teach' means to *give* knowledge and 'learn' means to *receive* it; 'lend' means to *give* something to someone temporarily and 'borrow' means to *receive* something temporarily].

Read the last sentence in the focus text. Ask the pupils to identify the word used incorrectly and to supply the correct choice ['less' should be 'fewer']. Explain that 'less' and 'fewer' are synonyms but in Standard English 'fewer' is used with countable plural nouns and 'less' with non-countable nouns with no plural. Invite the pupils to suggest the librarian's likely response [e.g. "You would prefer one with *fewer* pages?"]. Use this opportunity to revise other words that your pupils get confused [e.g. of/have; them/those; beat/win]. Use them to continue the focus text [e.g. "I might of read it," said the girl.].

EXTEND Discuss other word confusions [e.g. many people/much people; a number/an amount of pages].

PRACTISE

Pupil book page 40

APPLY

- The pupils create their own exchange of dialogue based on the focus text to show their knowledge of Standard/non-Standard word use.
- When they are editing their writing, remind the pupils to check their use of Standard English.
- The pupils write texts that will require use of the words discussed in the lesson [e.g. What did the Ancient Greeks teach us? Healthy eating – does it mean eating less?].

ASSESS

Dictation: Recent studies show that people now read <u>less</u> newspapers. Less time is spent reading newspapers; more time is spent viewing news on screen. What does this <u>learn</u> us?
Say: Underline and change the two non-Standard words.
Answer: fewer newspapers; teach us
Check: A full stop or a semicolon is used after the second 'newspapers', but not a comma.

Pupil book answers

Standard English: confusing words

Remember

The meanings of some words are often confused with each other, for example 'learn' and 'teach'. In **Standard English**, it is important to use the correct word.

Miss Li is learning us about grammar. ✗
Miss Li is teaching us about grammar. ✓

Try it

1 Complete each sentence using the correct word from the brackets.

The club may need to ___borrow___ some money from the bank.   (borrow lend)

Of course, I will ___lend___ you my guitar if you think it will help.   (borrow lend)

Some people say we should try to eat ___less___ meat.   (less fewer)

Write a summary of the main events using ___fewer___ words.   (less fewer)

This week, the instructor ___taught___ us how to dive.   (learnt taught)

At the end of a dramatic game, City ___beat___ United on penalties.   (won beat)

2 Rewrite these sentences using **Standard English** words.

I need to lend them books from you.	I need to borrow those books from you.
We should of won them easy.	We should have beaten them easily.
Lily and me learnt Aliyah how to swim.	Lily and I taught Aliyah how to swim.
Lucky, there was less mistakes this time.	Luckily, there were fewer mistakes this time.
Dad is learning me sister to drive proper.	Dad is teaching my sister to drive properly.

Sentence practice

Write a sentence using each pair of words: 'beat' and 'won'; 'teach' and 'learn'; 'less' and 'fewer'.

I beat my opponent and won the trophy.

Our teachers teach us and we learn.

The dentist told me to eat less sugar and fewer sweets.

40

As well as the words discussed in the lesson, these sentences also include a variety of non-Standard forms that are covered in earlier books [e.g. verbs; pronouns; adverbs].

Use this activity to pick up on any non-Standard words that your pupils use in their writing, and discuss the Standard form that should generally be used instead.

These are just examples of sentences the pupils might write to show the correct use of these words.

Lesson 30 Layout devices: tables

Focus using layout devices to structure and present text [e.g. tables; headings; sub-headings]

Key terms heading, sub-heading, **table**, **column**, bullet points

Focus text How the Olympic Games have grown

	1908	1948	2012
Nations	22	59	205
Athletes	2800	4104	12 500

TEACH

Show the focus text. Discuss the information given. Ask: How *have* the Olympic Games grown?

Ask the pupils why the writer has presented the information like this rather than as continuous prose [e.g. to make it easier for the reader to see how the numbers have grown]. Discuss what the focus text would be like as continuous prose [e.g. the numbers might get lost in the text].

Explain that we sometimes present information in a table like this rather than as continuous prose. It helps to organise the information concisely and makes it easy for the reader to follow or understand the most important points. Discuss what sort of information is best suited to this style of presentation [e.g. comparison of a number of things; information involving numbers or a lot of detail].

Use the focus text to discuss how a table is presented. Explain that a table needs a heading or title to tell the reader what the information is about [e.g. How the Olympic Games have grown]. The table columns should also have headings – in this case the three years being compared. Explain that it is important to present a table consistently [e.g. in the focus text, just numbers are used in the columns, but if the first entry said '22 nations', then the word 'nations' should be used in all the entries].

Ask the pupils to imagine that this was part of a longer text about the Olympic Games. What other layout devices might be used to help structure and present it? [e.g. headings; sub-headings; bullet points]

EXTEND Discuss other ways of presenting information [e.g. labelled diagrams; columns of text; graphs].

PRACTISE

Pupil book page 41

APPLY

- Ask the pupils to look at a completed piece of non-fiction writing. Discuss where a table or other presentational device might help to improve it.
- In other subject areas, the pupils present information in tables rather than as continuous prose [e.g. in science – to record measurements; in geography – to compare features or locations].
- The pupils plan a piece of writing to include a variety of layout devices [e.g. a report; a magazine article]. Discuss which information is best presented as a table, bullet points or in columns.

ASSESS

Dictation: A coach trip to Oxford costs £12 for adults, £6 for children and £10 for OAPs. A trip to Blackpool costs £15 for adults, £7 for children and £12 for OAPs. A trip to Bristol costs £16 for adults, £8 for children and £12.50 for OAPs.
Say: Present this information as a table.
Check: The information is presented clearly, accurately and consistently, with a suitable title; headed columns [e.g. Adults; Children] and consistent entries.

Pupil book answers

Layout devices: tables

Remember

Sometimes **columns**, **lists** or **tables** are used to organise information and present it concisely. This makes it easier for the reader to understand. A suitable title and column headings help to clarify what information is shown.

How the Olympic Games have grown

	1908	1948	2012
Nations	22	59	205
Athletes	2800	4104	12500

Try it

1 Complete this **table** of information about different foods.

Getting the right nutrients

Nutrient	Where are they found?	What do they do?
Proteins	fish, meat, eggs, cheese	aid growth and repair
Carbohydrates	bread, rice, pasta, cereals	give the body energy
Fats	oil, margarine, butter	store energy for use later

The table should be completed in a way that is consistent with the information already given [a list of foods with commas; sentence fragments to explain their role].

The pupils could refer to science resources or previous work if they need help.

2 Read the information below. Then present the information as a **table**.

The highest mountain in the world is Mount Everest, in the Himalayas on the border between Tibet and Nepal. It is 8850m high, although the heights of mountains do change over time. The second highest mountain is K2, at 8611m. It is on the border between China and Pakistan. The third highest mountain is on the border between India and Nepal. It is called Kanchenjunga and stands at 8597m.

The world's highest mountains

Mountain	Location	Height
Everest	Tibet/Nepal	8850m
K2	China/Pakistan	8611m
Kanchenjunga	India/Nepal	8597m

This gives an example of the completed table, with the information from the text accurately presented.

Check that the pupils have included suitable column headings and presented the information consistently [e.g. by giving the unit of measurement with each height, or alternatively including this in the headings [e.g. Height (m); Height in metres].

Sentence practice

Find some information about <u>three</u> or <u>four</u> different types of sea creature. On a separate piece of paper, organise and present this information as a **table**.

41

Check that the pupils have given their table a suitable title and chosen suitable column headings to show what features are being compared [e.g. size; diet; predators].

If you prefer, you could adapt this activity to use information from a current area of study.

Revision 3 answers

Focus: forming nouns with prefixes

Even if the pupils cannot remember the meanings of these prefixes, they should be able to deduce the meaning by thinking about the different word meanings and what they have in common.

This page focuses on revising vocabulary, particularly knowledge of prefixes and suffixes. The pupils should understand how prefixes and suffixes change the meaning or class of words.

The focus of each activity is given in case further revision is needed.

Revision 3

1 What does the **prefix anti–** mean in these **nouns?**

antidote   antiseptic   anti-gravity   antifreeze   against

What does the **prefix auto–** mean in these **nouns?**

autobiography   autograph   automaton   autopilot   self or own

Focus: forming verbs with prefixes [e.g. de–, mis–, re–, un–]

Alternative prefixes are acceptable as long as the new word makes sense in the sentence.

2 Add a **prefix** to each **verb** to change its meaning.

It is time to __re_discover these beautiful gardens.

The spy began to __de_code the message.

I __mis_understood what he said.

First, we need to __un_wind the ball of wool.

Help me __de_flate the air mattress.

Yesterday, the bath _over_flowed while I was on the phone.

Focus: forming adjectives with suffixes [e.g. –ful, –less]

The adjectives should be spelt correctly, including those that require a change in the spelling of the root word [e.g. noise/noisy].

3 Use a **suffix** to make each noun into an **adjective**. Write the adjective.

doubt	doubtful	glamour	glamorous
accident	accidental	time	timeless
noise	noisy	athlete	athletic
courage	courageous	metal	metallic

Focus: forming verbs with suffixes [e.g. –ate, –ise, –ify]

These are just examples of sentences using the given words. The verbs must be spelt correctly.

4 Write a sentence using a **verb** formed from each word shown in brackets.

It's easy to criticise when you haven't tried it yourself.   (critic)

Bees help to pollinate our crops.   (pollen)

She could not justify her reckless behaviour.   (just)

Dairy products help to strengthen your teeth.   (strength)

Let the chocolate pudding solidify in the fridge.   (solid)

5 Write a sentence using an **adverb** formed from the word 'fortunate'.

Fortunately, Mum had kept the receipt so we could take the shoes back.

42

Focus: forming adverbs with suffixes [–ly]

This is just an example of a correctly punctuated sentence using the adverb 'fortunately'. There should be a comma after the adverb if it is fronted.

This page revises punctuation and grammar introduced in **Grammar 5** and further developed in this book. The focus of each activity is given in case further revision is needed.

Schofield & Sims **Grammar and Punctuation**   Grammar 6

6 Insert <u>two</u> **commas** in each sentence below to indicate a **parenthesis**.

Leonardo da Vinci's most famous painting, called the Mona Lisa, is a portrait of a mysterious lady.

Hummingbirds, which are not much larger than a bumblebee, are brightly coloured birds that feed at flowers.

Name another **punctuation** mark that could be used in place of the commas in the sentences above.

_____brackets or two dashes_____

7 Complete each sentence by adding a **relative clause**. Use the correct punctuation.

Many tasks are now done by computers, which are much quicker.

We are raising money for a charity that provides shelter for homeless people.

8 Complete each sentence by adding a **subordinate clause** that gives a condition, starting with 'if' or 'unless'.

My little brother won't go to bed unless we leave the door open.

Some animals will not survive if they cannot adapt to the changing climate.

9 Rewrite each sentence to include a **parenthesis**.

Michelle was the youngest ever national champion.

Michelle, who was only sixteen at the time, was the youngest ever national champion.

The factory was closed down many years ago.

The factory, which was at the end of our street, was closed down many years ago.

10 Underline the **pronoun** that could lead to ambiguity in the passage below, and explain why.

Jess parked her car outside her house. <u>It</u> was new and she felt very proud.

'It' could refer to the car or the house.

43

Focus: punctuation to indicate a parenthesis

Remind the pupils that the rest of the sentence, either side of the parenthesis, should make sense without it.

Focus: relative clauses

These are just examples of relative clauses. Accept any relative clause that makes sense. The pupils should add a comma if the relative clause provides *non-essential* information.

Focus: subordinating conjunctions and subordinate clauses

These are just examples of conditional sentences using the conjunctions 'if' and 'unless' to form subordinate clauses. Accept any clause that provides a condition and makes sense in the context.

Focus: parenthesis

These are just examples. The sentences should be correctly punctuated with brackets, commas or dashes to indicate the parenthesis.

Focus: pronouns to aid cohesion and avoid ambiguity

You could discuss how to reword the sentence to avoid ambiguity [e.g. Jess felt very proud of her new car as she parked it outside her house.].

Writing task 3: Analysis sheet

Tick the circles to show amount of evidence found in writing:
1 No evidence
2 Some evidence
3 Clear evidence

Pupil name: _____

Date: _____

Assessing punctuation

The writing sample demonstrates:	Evidence		
sentence boundaries demarcated with appropriate end punctuation and capital letters used where necessary.	①	②	③
apostrophes used for contractions and possession.	①	②	③
inverted commas and internal punctuation used to correctly denote direct speech.	①	②	③
commas, brackets or dashes used to indicate a parenthesis.	①	②	③
commas, colons, semicolons, hyphens and dashes used correctly.	①	②	③

Assessing grammar and sentence structure

The writing sample demonstrates:	Evidence		
Standard English and formal/informal language and structures as appropriate.	①	②	③
variation in sentence types, sentence lengths and sentence openings including the use of multi-clause sentences.	①	②	③
relative clauses [including parentheses and omitted pronouns] to clarify, explain or add ideas.	①	②	③
varied verb forms [progressive and perfect] and appropriate choice of tense.	①	②	③
modal verbs and adverbs to express possibility [e.g. perhaps ...; it could be ...].	①	②	③
passive forms used for effect, such as to hide the agent.	①	②	③
expanded noun phrases to convey information concisely, and adverbials to add detail.	①	②	③
adverbs used to comment and add shades of meaning [e.g. Personally, ...; extremely dark].	①	②	③
pronouns chosen for clarity and to aid cohesion.	①	②	③

Key target: _____

Writing task 3: Pupil checklist

Name: _____   Date: _____

Reread what you have written to check that it makes sense. Tick the circle if you have correctly used the punctuation or grammar feature in your writing.

Punctuation

- ◯ I have used capital letters at the beginning of sentences and for proper nouns, and full stops, question marks or exclamation marks at the end of sentences.
- ◯ I have used capital letters for proper nouns.
- ◯ I have used apostrophes in contractions and for possession.
- ◯ I have used inverted commas and other punctuation in direct speech.
- ◯ I have used commas to separate phrases and clauses and to clarify meaning.
- ◯ I have used commas, brackets or dashes to indicate parenthesis in a sentence.
- ◯ I have used colons, semicolons and commas in lists.
- ◯ I have used colons, semicolons or single dashes between main clauses.
- ◯ I have used hyphens to avoid ambiguity.

Grammar and sentences

- ◯ I have written in Standard English and used formal or informal language and structures as appropriate.
- ◯ I have used varied sentence openings, sentence lengths and types of sentence, including some multi-clause sentences.
- ◯ I have used relative clauses to clarify, explain or add ideas.
- ◯ I have used different verb forms, including progressive and perfect forms, and the correct tense.
- ◯ I have used modal verbs and adverbs to suggest possibilities (e.g. might, perhaps).
- ◯ I have used adverbials to add detail, and expanded noun phrases to give precise information.
- ◯ I have used the passive voice for effect.
- ◯ I have used adverbs to comment and add shades of meaning (e.g. Personally, ..., extremely dark).
- ◯ I have used pronouns rather than repeating nouns.

Teacher feedback

[ ]

My key target: _____

Final test

Name: _____

1 Which word completes the sentence using **Standard English**? Tick <u>one</u> box.

She sings _____ .

beautiful ☐   lovely ☐   well ☐   good ☐

| 1 mark |

2 Complete the sentence using the **progressive form** of the verb 'laugh'.

They nearly fell over because they _____ so much.

| 1 mark |

3 Rewrite the statement below as a **question** using a **question tag**.

The tickets will arrive today.

_____

| 1 mark |

4 Which sentence uses all its **apostrophes** correctly? Tick <u>one</u> box.

I couldn't look at the other peoples' faces. ☐

The sun's shining and its' a lovely day. ☐

The captain's possessions were taken on to the pirates' ship. ☐

Those clothes' are your's, aren't they? ☐

| 1 mark |

5 What does the **root** 'nov–' mean in the **word family** below? Tick <u>one</u> box.

(novelty   innovate   novice   novel)

now ☐   next ☐   new ☐   none ☐

| 1 mark |

6 Underline all the **determiners** in the sentence below.

Break one egg into a bowl and slowly stir in the flour and some milk until you have a smooth batter.

1 mark

7 Tick <u>one</u> box in each row to show whether the underlined word is a **preposition** or an **adverb**.

Sentence	Preposition	Adverb
I told him to wait <u>outside</u>.		
She waited <u>outside</u> the school gates.		
It took me <u>over</u> a week to finish.		
He slipped on a banana skin and fell <u>over</u>.		

1 mark

8 Underline the longest possible **noun phrase** in the sentence below.

The film ends with a thrilling car chase through the streets of London.

1 mark

9 Rewrite the sentence below so that it begins with the **adverbial**. Punctuate your sentence correctly.

He opened the door without thinking.

_____

1 mark

10 Underline the <u>two</u> words in the sentence below that are **antonyms** of each other.

The criminals tried to conceal the evidence but it did not take the police long to reveal their true identity and return the missing items.

1 mark

11 Label the boxes '**subject**' and '**object**' to show the parts of the sentence.

<u>The cat</u> chased <u>the pigeon</u>.

↑   ↑

[   ]   [   ]

[   ]
1 mark

12 Draw lines to match the pairs of words that are **synonyms** of each other.

substantial   bewilder

present   insignificant

confuse   considerable

unimportant   current

[   ]
1 mark

13 Rewrite the sentence below so that it is written in the **passive voice**.

The guide took us to the dungeon.

_____

[   ]
1 mark

14 Present this information as **bullet points**. Punctuate your answer correctly.

The new clubs starting this term are a chess club, a computer club and a film club.

We have _____

_____

_____

_____

[   ]
1 mark

15 Rewrite these two sentences as <u>one</u> sentence, using a **semicolon**.

Outside, the two houses were identical. Inside, they were completely different.

_____

[   ]
1 mark

16 Tick <u>one</u> box to show where a **dash** should go in the sentence below.

She looked at the alarm clock through her sleepy eyes it was half past nine.

1 mark

17 Rewrite the sentence below using **ellipsis** to avoid repetition.

I don't think the road will flood but it might flood.

1 mark

18 Insert a **colon** and <u>two</u> **commas** into the sentence below.

Dad threw everything into the skip broken toys cardboard boxes an old carpet and Joe's old bike.

1 mark

19 Explain how the use of a **hyphen** changes the meaning in these two sentences.

I have a little used pushchair for sale.

I have a little-used pushchair for sale.

1 mark

20 Complete the sentence below so that it uses the **subjunctive form**.

If it _____ possible, I would be most grateful.

1 mark

End of test

Final test: Mark scheme

Q	Focus	Answer
1	Standard English: adverbs	**Award 1 mark** for the correct word ticked. well ✓
2	past progressive form; tense consistency	**Award 1 mark** for the correct verb form. were laughing As the sentence begins in the past tense, the answer must use the past progressive for tense consistency.
3	grammatical patterns: questions and question tags	**Award 1 mark** for a correctly punctuated question using a question tag. The tickets will arrive today, won't they? The comma and apostrophe should also be correctly placed.
4	apostrophes for possession and omission [in contractions]	**Award 1 mark** for the correct sentence ticked. The captain's possessions were taken on to the pirates' ship. ✓
5	word families	**Award 1 mark** for the correct word ticked. new ✓
6	determiners	**Award 1 mark** for all <u>five</u> determiners correctly identified. Break <u>one</u> egg into <u>a</u> bowl and slowly stir in <u>the</u> flour and <u>some</u> milk until you have <u>a</u> smooth batter.
7	prepositions and adverbs	**Award 1 mark** for a correctly completed table.

Question 7 table

Sentence	Preposition	Adverb
I told him to wait <u>outside</u>.		✓
She waited <u>outside</u> the school gates.	✓	
It took me <u>over</u> a week to finish.	✓	
He slipped on a banana skin and fell <u>over</u>.		✓

Q	Focus	Answer
8	expanded noun phrases	**Award 1 mark** for the correct part of the sentence underlined. The film ends with <u>a thrilling car chase through the streets of London</u>. The determiner and full prepositional phrase must be included.
9	adverbials; commas after fronted adverbials	**Award 1 mark** for a correctly punctuated sentence. Without thinking, he opened the door.
10	antonyms	**Award 1 mark** for <u>both</u> words correctly underlined. The criminals tried to <u>conceal</u> the evidence but it did not take the police long to <u>reveal</u> their true identity and return the missing items.
11	grammatical terms: subject and object	**Award 1 mark** for <u>both</u> boxes correctly labelled. <u>The cat</u> chased <u>the pigeon</u>. subject object

12	synonyms; formal vocabulary	**Award 1 mark** for all <u>four</u> pairs correctly matched.
		substantial — bewilder present — insignificant confuse — considerable unimportant — current
13	passive voice	**Award 1 mark** for a correctly punctuated sentence using the passive voice. We were taken to the dungeon (by the guide). The phrase 'by the guide' may be omitted.
14	punctuation of bullet points	**Award 1 mark** for a consistently punctuated list, e.g. We have three new clubs starting this term: ● a chess club ● a computer club ● a film club Accept capitalisation and the use of commas/semicolons at the end of items in the list, as long as it is consistent and the last item ends with a full stop.
15	semicolon between main clauses	**Award 1 mark** for a correctly punctuated sentence. Outside, the two houses were identical; inside, they were completely different. There should be no capital letter after the semicolon.
16	dash between main clauses	**Award 1 mark** for the correct box ticked. She looked at the alarm clock through her sleepy eyes – it was half past nine. ✓
17	ellipsis	**Award 1 mark** for a correctly punctuated sentence. I don't think the road will flood but it might.
18	colons to introduce lists; commas in lists	**Award 1 mark** for the colon and <u>both</u> commas correctly inserted. Dad threw everything into the skip: broken toys, cardboard boxes, an old carpet and Joe's old bike. There should be no additional comma before 'and'.
19	hyphens to avoid ambiguity	**Award 1 mark** for an explanation of the meaning of the two sentences, e.g. Without the hyphen, it means that the pushchair is small and second-hand. With the hyphen, it means that the pushchair has not been used very much. Answers must explain the specific effect on the meaning. *Do not accept* answers that merely explain the function of a hyphen [e.g. 'The hyphen shows that the words go together.'].
20	subjunctive verb form	**Award 1 mark** for the correct word. were

Final test: Analysis sheet

Tick the box for each correct answer.

Q	Focus	Pupil names									
1	Standard English: adverbs										
2	past progressive form; tense consistency										
3	grammatical patterns: questions and question tags										
4	apostrophes for possession and omission [in contractions]										
5	word families										
6	determiners										
7	prepositions and adverbs										
8	expanded noun phrases										
9	adverbials; commas after fronted adverbials										
10	antonyms										
11	grammatical terms: subject and object										
12	synonyms; formal vocabulary										
13	passive voice										
14	punctuation of bullet points										
15	semicolon between main clauses										
16	dash between main clauses										
17	ellipsis										
18	colons to introduce lists; commas in lists										
19	hyphens to avoid ambiguity										
20	subjunctive verb form										
Total correct answers per pupil											

Target tracking sheet

Group: _____

Target: _____

Date set: _____ Date for review: _____

Pupil name	Evidence from independent writing	Progress in independent writing
		① ② ③
		① ② ③
		① ② ③
		① ② ③
		① ② ③
		① ② ③
		① ② ③
		① ② ③
		① ② ③
		① ② ③

Learning pathways sheet

Pupil name: _____

Date last updated: _____

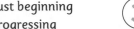
Punctuation pathway

Use commas to mark clauses or phrases and to clarify meaning.
① ② ③

Use inverted commas and other punctuation to indicate direct speech.
① ② ③

Use apostrophes for contractions and possession.
① ② ③

Use brackets, dashes, commas to indicate parenthesis.
① ② ③

Use colons, semicolons, commas in sentences with lists.
① ② ③

Punctuate bullet points consistently.
① ② ③

Use hyphens to avoid ambiguity.
① ② ③

Use colons, semicolons, dashes between main clauses.
① ② ③

Grammar and sentence pathway

Use Standard English and formal/informal language as appropriate.
① ② ③

Vary sentence types, openings, lengths.
① ② ③

Use verb tenses accurately, including progressive and perfect forms.
① ② ③

Use expanded noun phrases for description and concision, and adverbials to add detail.
① ② ③

Use a variety of relative clauses to clarify and explain.
① ② ③

Use pronouns for clarity and cohesion.
① ② ③

Use the passive voice to change or maintain focus.
① ② ③

Use modal verbs and adverbs for shades of meaning.
① ② ③

Glossary

Adjective

An **adjective** is a word used to modify or specify a noun [e.g. an <u>angry</u> man; the <u>red</u> car].
- Some adjectives are formed by adding a suffix to a word [e.g. care<u>ful</u>; care<u>less</u>].
- Some adjectives are formed by adding both a suffix and a prefix [e.g. <u>un</u>remark<u>able</u>].

Active and passive voice

In the **active voice**, the subject of the sentence performs the action of the verb [e.g. <u>The dog chased</u> the man.]. In the **passive voice**, the sentence is turned round and the receiver of the action becomes the subject of the sentence [e.g. <u>The man was chased</u> by the dog.]. Lessons 3, 4 and 13

Adverb

An **adverb** is a word that modifies a verb or action in a sentence. An adverb can specify *how, where,* or *when* the action took place [e.g. He arrived <u>quietly</u>. He arrived <u>outside</u>. He arrived <u>yesterday</u>.]. Sometimes adverbs modify other words, such as another adverb [e.g. <u>really</u> quickly] or an adjective [e.g. a <u>really</u> good idea].
- Some adverbs [and **adverbials**] are used to show links between events [e.g. 'therefore' shows the result of an action]. They help to link sentences and paragraphs and achieve text cohesion. Lesson 15
- Some adverbs express how likely an event is [e.g. 'surely' – very likely; 'perhaps' – a possibility].
- Some adverbs comment on the whole sentence or clause [e.g. <u>Fortunately,</u> the rain stopped.].

Adverbial

An **adverbial** is a word, phrase or clause that is used like an adverb – it adds more detail about a verb or event in a sentence. Adverbs can be used as adverbials, as can phrases, including prepositional phrases [e.g. He arrived <u>in a hurry</u>.] or noun phrases [e.g. He arrived <u>last night</u>.]. Subordinate clauses starting with conjunctions can also be adverbials [e.g. He arrived <u>after I left</u>.]. Lesson 1
- **Fronted adverbials** are adverbial words, phrases or clauses used at the start of a sentence [e.g. <u>Suddenly</u>, the ghost appeared. <u>In the morning</u>, I lay in bed. <u>Although the sun was rising</u>, he slept on.]. Commas are always used after fronted adverbials to separate them from the rest of the sentence.

Ambiguity

Ambiguity occurs when there is more than one possible meaning, for example when it is not clear who or what a pronoun refers to [e.g. He dropped the computer on his leg and it broke.].
- Sometimes punctuation is needed to help avoid ambiguity. For example, commas or hyphens can help to clarify the meaning of a sentence [e.g. 'Keep tackling, Joe.' rather than 'Keep tackling Joe.'; 'We must re-cover this sofa.' rather than 'We must recover this sofa.']. Lesson 20

Apostrophe

An **apostrophe [']** is a punctuation mark with two different uses:
- it shows the position of missing letters in **contractions** or shortened forms of words that are often used in informal speech [e.g. can't; who's; we've]. Lessons 9 and 11
- it is used with the letter 's' in the **possessive** form of nouns [e.g. Sam's hat; both boys' coats].

Clause

A **clause** is a group of words that are connected together and include a verb. A clause can be a complete sentence or part of a sentence.

- A **main clause** is a clause that makes sense independently [e.g. He paused.]. A sentence always contains at least one main clause, and can contain more than one if the clauses are linked with a co-ordinating conjunction [He paused <u>and</u> then he spoke.]. Lessons 1, 17 and 24
- A **subordinate clause** is a less important clause that is added to a main clause, for example by using a subordinating conjunction. It adds extra detail [e.g. He paused <u>before he spoke</u>.]. The subordinate clause 'before he spoke' does not make sense without the main clause. Lessons 1 and 24
- A **relative clause** is a type of subordinate clause. It usually adds more detail about the noun, although it can comment on a whole clause. Relative clauses begin with a relative pronoun, which refers back to someone or something already mentioned [e.g. The king wore a crown **<u>that</u>** <u>was made of tin</u>.]. Sometimes the relative pronoun is omitted [e.g. The king wore a crown <u>made of tin</u>.]. Lessons 1, 2 and 24

Cohesion

A text has **cohesion** when it is clear how the parts fit together. Linking adverbials, pronouns and the use of repeated words and phrases can all help to achieve this. Lesson 15

Colons and semicolons

Colons [:] and **semicolons [;]** are punctuation marks used within sentences. They can be used to separate two main clauses within a sentence. A single dash can also be used in this way. Lessons 17 and 18 Colons and semicolons are also used in sentences with lists or in a list of bullet points. A colon is used after a main clause that introduces a list. Semicolons are used to separate lists of longer phrases. Lessons 5 and 6

Comma

A **comma [,]** is a punctuation mark used to separate different parts of a sentence, for example:

- to separate the items in a list [e.g. She put the fresh eggs, a packet of cheese and some butter in the basket.]. Lesson 5
- to separate spoken words from non-spoken words in direct speech [e.g. "I'm hungry," he said.].
- to separate a fronted adverbial from the rest of the sentence [e.g. In the forest, the wolf howled.].
- to indicate a parenthesis in a sentence [e.g. Jamie's mother, who was a great cook, had been baking all day.]. Lessons 2 and 24
- to avoid ambiguity and make the meaning of a sentence clear [e.g. Keep tackling, Joe.]. Lesson 25

Conditional sentence

In a **conditional sentence**, one thing depends on another. A conditional sentence has a main clause and a subordinate clause that gives a condition. The subordinate clause often begins with the conjunction 'if' and gives the condition. Sometimes the conjunction 'unless' is used.

Conjunction

A **conjunction** is a word that joins two words, phrases or clauses together. Conjunctions show how ideas link together [e.g. 'because' shows cause; 'when', 'while' and 'until' show time links; 'but' and 'although' show contrast]. Lessons 1 and 24

There are two types of conjunction:

- **Co-ordinating conjunctions** [and, but, or] link together two words, phrases or clauses that are equally important [e.g. Bill <u>and</u> Diane were looking for a house <u>or</u> a flat. Bill preferred a house <u>but</u> Diane wanted a flat.]. Lesson 24

- **Subordinating conjunctions** [e.g. because; when; while] introduce a subordinate or less important clause [e.g. Bill preferred to live in a house <u>because</u> he wanted a garden.]. Lesson 24

Determiner

A **determiner** is the word that is used before a noun [e.g. <u>a</u> cat; <u>this</u> dog]. In a noun phrase, the determiner comes before any adjectives [e.g. <u>a</u> little cat; <u>this</u> big dog]. It helps to specify the noun as known [e.g. <u>my</u> school; <u>this</u> school] or unknown [e.g. <u>a</u> school; <u>some</u> schools]. Lesson 15

- **Articles** ['the', 'a' and 'an'] are the most common determiners. 'The' is the definite article. It shows that the noun that it precedes is known [e.g. <u>the</u> dog]. 'A' and 'an' are indefinite articles. They show that the noun they precede is unknown [e.g. <u>a</u> cat; <u>an</u> elephant]. 'An' is used before a word beginning with a vowel sound.
- Many other words can also be used as determiners, including demonstratives [e.g. this], possessives [e.g. your] and quantifiers [e.g. some]. Some of these words can also be used in other ways, for example as pronouns but they are determiners when followed by a noun or noun phrase.

Direct and indirect speech

Direct speech records what someone says using the speaker's original words. **Indirect speech** reports what was said but it does not use the exact words of the speaker.

- **Inverted commas**, sometimes called **speech marks**, are used to mark the beginning and end of the spoken words in direct speech [e.g. "My name is Jack."]. Direct speech is often followed by a reporting clause [unspoken words that say who is speaking]. A comma separates the spoken words from the unspoken words [e.g. "My name is Jack," said the boy.]. If the spoken words are a question or an exclamation, then a question mark or exclamation mark is used instead of the comma.
- If the unspoken words come first, a comma is used to separate the unspoken words from the spoken words [e.g. Maya said, "Listen to that."]. If the unspoken words are placed in the middle of a spoken sentence, two commas are needed [e.g. "I heard it before," said Maya, "but this time it's louder."].

Ellipsis

Ellipsis is omitting words that are expected or predictable in order to avoid repetition [e.g. You can take off and ~~you can~~ land.]. Lesson 16

An ellipsis is also a punctuation mark [...] used to show an omission or to leave a sentence deliberately unfinished. Lesson 26

Hyphen

A **hyphen** [-] is a punctuation mark used to link words together [e.g. fun-filled]. Hyphens can help to avoid ambiguity [e.g. recover the book; re-cover the book]. Lesson 20

Layout devices

Layout devices are methods of setting out text so that it is easy for the reader to follow or access the information. For example:

- Headings and sub-headings show the subject of the text that follows.
- A list of bullet points is easy for the reader to follow. Lesson 6
- A table presents detailed information concisely so the reader can easily pick out the key points. Lesson 30

Noun

Nouns are words that name things, people and places [e.g. car; park; man; day]. These are examples of **common nouns**.

- **Proper nouns** are the names of specific people, places, things [e.g. Joe Henson; Banbury Park; February]. Proper nouns start with a capital letter.
- An **abstract noun** is a noun that does not describe a person, place or thing but rather names an idea, quality, or state [e.g. bravery; willingness]. These words are often formed by adding suffixes to adjectives. Lesson 22
- Many nouns have singular and plural forms. '**Singular**' means just one; '**plural**' means more than one [e.g. cat/cats]. Non-countable nouns do not have a plural form [e.g. butter]. Lesson 22
- A **collective noun** refers to a whole group of things [e.g. a class of children].
- A **noun phrase** is a group of words built around a noun. An expanded noun phrase might include a determiner, adjective[s], nouns and/or prepositional phrases [e.g. the fast police car with flashing lights].

Paragraph

A **paragraph** is a group of sentences that go together because they have one main idea or theme. Paragraphs are used to organise ideas in writing. Lesson 15

Parenthesis

A **parenthesis** is a word, phrase or clause that is inserted into a sentence to add extra information. **Brackets**, **dashes** or **commas** are used to separate the parenthesis from the rest of the sentence [e.g. Jamie Brown (my best friend) is a talented football player.]. Lessons 2 and 24

Phrase

A **phrase** is a group of words that are connected together.

- A **noun phrase** is a group of words [e.g. determiners; adjectives; prepositional phrases] built around a noun.
- A **prepositional phrase** is a group of words starting with a preposition [e.g. under the bridge].

Prefix

A **prefix** is a group of letters added to the start of an existing word to make another word. Adding a prefix changes the meaning of the original word, for example changing the meaning of adjectives or verbs [e.g <u>un</u>pleasant, <u>dis</u>honest; <u>un</u>do, <u>re</u>connect, <u>over</u>load].

- Some prefixes create negative meanings or antonyms [e.g. <u>un</u>welcome; <u>dis</u>agree]. Lesson 8
- Other prefixes have specific meanings [e.g. <u>sub</u>marine – 'sub' means 'under'].
- Sometimes a hyphen is needed when adding a prefix to avoid ambiguity [e.g. re-cover the sofa]. Lesson 20

Preposition

A **preposition** is a word that shows how one thing relates to another in terms of place [e.g. <u>behind</u> the tree], time [e.g. <u>during</u> dinner] or cause [e.g. <u>due to</u> the weather].

- A preposition is always followed by a noun, pronoun or noun phrase and this creates a **prepositional phrase** [e.g. before breakfast; before him; before the storm]. This is important because some words, such as 'before', can also act as conjunctions.

Pronoun

A **pronoun** is a word that stands in place of a noun, proper noun or noun phrase. We use them to avoid repetition and improve cohesion. Lesson 15

- **Personal pronouns** are the most commonly used pronouns [e.g. he/him; they/them].
- **Possessive pronouns** are used to show possession [e.g. This pencil is mine.].
- **Relative pronouns** [who, whose, which, that] are used at the start of relative clauses. Lessons 1 and 2
- **Reflexive pronouns** are used to refer back to the subject, [e.g. myself; himself].
- **Indefinite pronouns** are used when the noun in unknown [e.g. someone].
- **Determiners** can also be used as pronouns when they stand in place of a noun [e.g. This is mine.].

Overuse of pronouns can lead to ambiguity about who or what the pronoun refers to.

Sentence

A **sentence** is a group of words put together to say something that makes sense. A sentence starts with a capital letter and ends with a full stop [.], question mark [?] or exclamation mark [!].
A sentence may consist of one clause or more than one clause [a **multi-clause sentence**]. Lessons 1 and 24
There are different forms of sentence with different functions and different grammatical patterns.

- **Statements** give information. They usually start with a subject followed by a verb [e.g. Joe ran away.].
- **Questions** ask for information and need a response. They can be formed using a question word [e.g. What is the weather like today?], a subject–verb reversal [e.g. Is it cold today?] or a question tag [e.g. It is cold today, isn't it?].
- **Commands** direct someone to do something. The main clause starts with a verb [e.g. Come here.].
- **Exclamations** express strong emotions and end with an exclamation mark. A strict definition of an exclamation refers to sentences starting with 'What' or 'How' [e.g. What a surprise! How amazing!]. However, **interjections** are also exclamatory [e.g. Oh dear!].
- Exclamation marks are sometimes added to other sentences to make exclamatory statements [e.g. It was great!] or exclamatory commands [e.g. Stop right there!]. However, this does not change the form of the sentence.

Sentence punctuation

Sentence punctuation refers to the use of capital letters and full stops to show the boundaries between sentences. It is an important part of punctuation as it helps to make the meaning of a text clear.

- A **question mark [?]** is used in place of a full stop if a sentence is a question.
- An **exclamation mark [!]** is used for exclamations or to show strong feeling.
- **Capital letters** are also used at the start of names and for the word 'I'.

Standard English

Standard English is the form of English usually used in writing or formal speech. Non-Standard English is sometimes used in informal or local speech. Non-Standard English is shown in the use of verb forms [e.g. 'I done it.' rather than 'I did it.'; 'We was late.' rather than 'We were late.'], pronouns [e.g. 'me brother and me went' rather than 'my brother and I went'] and adverbs [e.g. 'He ran quick.' rather than 'He ran quickly.']. Slang or colloquial words are also non-Standard English [e.g. nab/pinch]. Lessons 9, 10 and 29

Subject and object

A short sentence has a **subject** [who/what it is about] and a verb [e.g. The man ran.]. Lessons 3 and 4
Some sentences have a subject, a verb and an **object** [the person or thing affected by the action] [e.g. The man kicked the ball.]. Lessons 3 and 4

Subjunctive

The **subjunctive** is a special form of verb used in some sentence structures in formal language [e.g. I propose that he <u>apologise</u>.] and a few everyday expressions [e.g. If I <u>were</u> you...]. Lesson 14

Suffix

A **suffix** is a group of letters added to the end of an existing word to make another word. Suffixes often change words into different word classes [e.g. forming adjectives – 'wonder<u>ful</u>', 'power<u>less</u>', 'fam<u>ous</u>'; nouns – 'captiv<u>ity</u>', 'entertain<u>ment</u>'; or verbs – 'solid<u>ify</u>']. Lesson 22

Synonyms and antonyms

Synonyms are words with the same or similar meanings [e.g. 'glad' and 'happy']. Lesson 7
Antonyms are words with opposite meanings [e.g. 'good' and 'evil']. Lesson 8

Verb

A **verb** is a 'doing' or 'being' word. Verbs tell us about the actions in a sentence.

- Verbs also show **tense**. The tense tells us *when* the action happened – in the past or present. Many past-tense verbs are formed by adding –ed [e.g. waited; stopped; hurried]. Some verbs have irregular past-tense forms [e.g. see/saw; forget/forgot].
- Sometimes additional verbs, called **auxiliary verbs**, are used in a sentence alongside the main verb. These are 'helper' verbs [e.g. <u>has</u> come; <u>is</u> going].
- **Progressive forms** [also called continuous forms] can be used in the present and past tense to describe events that are, or were, in progress for some time. They use the –ing form of the verb with the helper [or auxiliary] verb 'am/are/is' in the present tense or 'was/were' in the past tense [e.g. He <u>is</u> sing<u>ing</u>. She <u>was</u> walk<u>ing</u>.]. Lesson 27
- **Perfect forms** are used to show time-and-cause relationships. The **present perfect form** of a verb is used to refer to events in the past, particularly when an event that began in the past is ongoing or still has consequences now [e.g. The tent <u>has started</u> to leak.]. It is formed using the helper [or auxiliary] verb 'has/have'. The **past perfect form**, formed using 'had', is used to refer back to an event that took place earlier [e.g. He <u>had arrived</u> before we got there.]. Lessons 27 and 28
- **Modal verbs** are auxiliary verbs that modify the meaning of other verbs, for example in order to show possibility or certainty [e.g. <u>might</u> come; <u>must</u> come].
- The English language has no specific future tense. Events in the future can be referred to using the present tense and modal verbs [e.g. I will do that tomorrow.]. Lesson 28

Word class

Every word belongs to a **word class**. The word class shows how the word is used. The main word classes are noun, verb, adjective, adverb, pronoun, conjunction, preposition and determiner.

- **Homonyms** are words that sound the same and are spelt the same but have different meanings. This means they can belong in different word classes. The context in which a word is used in a particular sentence determines its meaning and which word class it belongs to [e.g. He did <u>well</u>. He fetched water from the <u>well</u>.]. Lesson 21

Word family

Words in the same **word family** are related by meaning and how they are formed. They share the same **root word** [e.g. family, familiar] or a common root [e.g. horror, horrible].

- A root word is a stand-alone word without any prefixes or suffixes added to it [e.g. 'build' is the root word of 'builder', 'rebuild', 'building'].